SHANNON HAL

# BEST FRIENDS

Artwork by
LEUYEN PHAM

Color by HILARY SYCAMORE

First Second
New York

FOR CONNIE HSU,

THE THIRD MEMBER OF OUR SUPER BEST FRIENDS TRIO

PUBLISHED BY FIRST SECOND
FIRST SECOND IS AN IMPRINT OF ROARING BROOK PRESS,
A DIVISION OF HOLTZBRINCK PUBLISHING HOLDINGS LIMITED PARTNERSHIP
120 BROADWAY, NEW YORK, NY 10271

DON'T MISS YOUR NEXT FAVORITE BOOK FROM FIRST SECOND! FOR THE LATEST UPDATES GO TO FIRSTSECONDNEWSLETTER.COM AND SIGN UP FOR OUR ENEWSLETTER.



LIBRARY OF CONGRESS CONTROL NUMBER: 2018953553

PAPERBACK ISBN: 978-1-250-31746-9
HARDCOVER ISBN: 978-1-250-31745-2

OUR BOOKS MAY BE PURCHASED IN BULK FOR PROMOTIONAL, EDUCATIONAL, OR BUSINESS USE. PLEASE CONTACT YOUR LOCAL BOOKSELLER OR THE MACMILLAN CORPORATE AND PREMIUM SALES DEPARTMENT AT (800) 221-7945 EXT. 5442 OR BY EMAIL AT MACMILLANSPECIALMARKETS@MACMILLAN.COM.

FIRST EDITION, 2019
BOOK DESIGN BY LEUYEN PHAM, ANDREW ARNOLD, AND MOLLY JOHANSON

PRINTED IN THE UNITED STATES OF AMERICA BY WORZALLA, STEVENS POINT, WISCONSIN

THE ART IN THIS BOOK WAS RENDERED IN CROQUILLE AND INDIA BLACK INK AND DIGITALLY COLORED.

PAPERBACK: 10 9 8 7 6 5 4 3 2 1
HARDCOVER: 10 9 8 7 6 5 4 3 2 1

# Chapter One

Do you want to be best friends?

- ☐ YES!
- ☐ No
- ☐ Maybe

IN SUMMER, NOTHING EVER SEEMED TO CHANGE.

THE SKY STAYED BLUE.
THE AIR STAYED WARM.

AND FRIENDS STAYED
FRIENDS FOREVER.

SEE YOU LATER?
YEP!

SALT LAKE CITY, UTAH, 1985

THE SUMMER BEFORE SIXTH GRADE, I HAD MY FIRST JOB.

THE SCHOOL LIBRARIAN PAID ME A DOLLAR AN HOUR TO CHECK THE BOOKS.

AND SHE DIDN'T MIND IF I PAUSED TO SMELL THEM.

SHE EVEN BOUGHT ME A SODA.
TEACHERS' LOUNGE
Coca-Cola
ON A BREAK FROM WORK, SITTING IN THE TEACHERS' LOUNGE...

...FOR THE FIRST TIME I FELT LIKE I WASN'T QUITE A KID ANYMORE.
COL

THE PAST YEARS HAD BEEN ROUGH AT TIMES...

...BUT I WAS GOING INTO SIXTH GRADE.
NO ENTRY
STOP
FROM NOW ON, EVERYTHING WAS GOING TO BE FINE.

I MADE FOUR DOLLARS TODAY. THAT'LL BUY A LOT OF CANDY FOR OUR SCHOOL LOCKER.

THAT'S SO RAD.

REALLY? AWESOME!
WE'RE GOING TO HAVE THE BEST CLASS.
SIXTH GRADE IS GOING TO BE RAD.

SO RAD!
FINALLY, WE'LL BE THE QUEENS OF THE SCHOOL!

OOH, I LOVE THIS SONG!

ME TOO!
THE SUN ALWAYS SHINES...
I'VE NEVER HEARD IT BEFORE.

...ON T.V....

THE SUN ALWAYS SHINES ON T.V....
DOES EVERYONE KNOW THIS SONG EXCEPT ME?

LORD, I'M FIVE HUNDRED MILES FROM HOME...
GROWING UP, I MOSTLY LISTENED TO FOLK MUSIC...

...AND BLUEGRASS.
WILL THE CIRCLE BE UNBROKEN...

I ALSO KNEW MY OLDER SISTERS' MUSIC, BUT THEY WEREN'T THE SAME SONGS MY FRIENDS SEEMED TO KNOW.
PENNY LANE

I'D BEEN TRYING TO LEARN THE POPULAR SONGS, BUT I HAD A LOT OF CATCHING UP TO DO.

THIS YEAR, I WAS DETERMINED NOT TO BE LEFT OUT.

NOT IN ANY WAY.

ALL SHE WANTS TO DO IS...

ALL SHE WANTS TO DO IS DANCE!!!

OH NO, DID I
DO IT WRONG?
AM I BEING STUPID?

THE ARM WAVE... IN A CHAIN! EVEN COOLER!

SIXTH GRADE!
WE WERE THE OLDEST KIDS AT WASATCH ELEMENTARY.

JEN HAD ALWAYS BEEN THE MOST POPULAR GIRL IN OUR GRADE.
BUT NOW THAT WE WERE THE OLDEST IN THE SCHOOL, SHE WAS THE MOST POPULAR GIRL—

PERIOD.

I BROUGHT SUGAR BABIES AND STARBURSTS.

I BROUGHT GUMMY BERRIES, NERDS, DR PEPPER GUM...
ALSO...
IN THIRD, FOURTH, AND FIFTH GRADES, JEN SHARED A LOCKER WITH HER OLD BEST FRIEND.

BUT THIS YEAR, SHE CHOSE ME.
MY SISTER WENDY GAVE ME THIS BILLY IDOL POSTER.
COOL.

SO BASICALLY...
...I WAS BEST FRIENDS WITH THE QUEEN OF THE ENTIRE SCHOOL.
OOOOOOH!
AAAAAAAAH!
OHHHHHH!

HI SARAH!
HI EMILY.

JENNY HAD BULLIED ME FOR YEARS.

HI JENNY.
HI.

AT THE END OF FIFTH GRADE, I TOLD HER SHE COULDN'T BE A PART OF OUR GROUP ANYMORE.

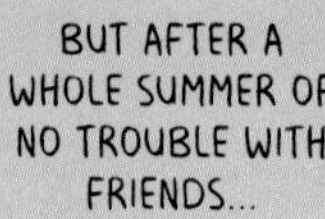
BUT AFTER A WHOLE SUMMER OF NO TROUBLE WITH FRIENDS...

...I WAS FEELING BRAVE.

AND I WANTED TO BE KIND.
I HOPE YOU HAD A GOOD SUMMER.
YEAH. YOU TOO.

MAYBE HAVING JENNY IN OUR NEW GROUP WOULD BE OKAY.

MAYBE SHE WOULDN'T BE MEAN TO ME ANYMORE.

I WAS THINKING, WE COULD BE THE SUPERHEROES OF THE PLAYGROUND, LOOK OUT FOR LITTLER KIDS, PROTECT THEM FROM BULLIES AND STUFF.
COOL.

IT WAS THE NEW GROUP!
I HEARD KIKI MOVED HERE FROM NEW YORK CITY!
KIKI IS COOL. SHE COULD BE PART OF OUR GROUP.
YEAH!

BETTER THAN BEFORE!

UGH, IT'S SO CROWDED.
STAY TOGETHER! LET'S MAKE A CHAIN!

WE COULD GET EVERYONE TO JOIN AND SEE HOW LONG WE CAN MAKE THE CHAIN.
LET'S JUST STICK WITH THE GROUP.

IT FELT PRETTY AMAZING.
FINALLY, I FELT LIKE I HAD REAL FRIENDS. FINALLY, I FELT LIKED.

MORE THAN LIKED.
POPULAR.

NOT ONLY WAS JEN MY NEW BEST FRIEND, BUT NICOLE, AMY, AND I WERE REALLY CLOSE.
WE SHOULD MAKE UP A SECRET HANDSHAKE.
YEAH, AND CODE NAMES!

THE THREE OF US WERE WORKING ON A GROUP PROJECT.
LIBRARIAN OFFICE

FOR A WHOLE WEEK, OUR TEACHER LET US SPEND AN HOUR EACH DAY ALONE IN THE LIBRARY.
WHERE'S AMY?
OH, SHE HAD TO HELP OUT WITH SOMETHING ELSE.

SO, WHAT DO YOU THINK ABOUT AMY?

I LIKE HER. WHY?
AMY HIDING FROM ME

SHE BUGS ME SOMETIMES. DOESN'T SHE BUG YOU TOO?

NOT REALLY. I THINK SHE'S NICE.

REALLY?
YEAH...

WELL...DON'T TELL HER WHAT I SAID.

LATER...
HEY AMY. TOO BAD YOU COULDN'T COME TO THE LIBRARY TODAY.
IT'S OKAY.

SO WHAT DID YOU GUYS TALK ABOUT?
UM...
NOTHING.

I SPENT A COUPLE OF DAYS SUPER WORRIED, TRYING TO KEEP AMY FROM FINDING OUT THAT NICOLE DIDN'T LIKE HER SO MUCH.

HEY SHANNON...

...WE'VE GOT SOMETHING TO TELL YOU.

THEY'D TRICKED ME TO SEE IF I WOULD TALK ABOUT AMY BEHIND HER BACK.
SOMEONE TOLD US STUFF ABOUT YOU.

WE JUST WANTED TO MAKE SURE YOU WERE REALLY OUR FRIEND.
AND YOU ARE!
JUST THEN, I DIDN'T CARE THAT THEY'D SET ME UP.

I WAS JUST RELIEVED THAT
I'D PASSED THEIR TEST!

BUT...

...WHO HAD TOLD THEM STUFF ABOUT ME?

I HAD FRIENDS. BUT IN SIXTH GRADE, IT GOT
TRICKIER TO KNOW HOW TO KEEP THEM.

IT SEEMED LIKE AS SOON AS I FIGURED STUFF OUT...
HUMMING to the song "STRAY CATS"

I DON'T REALLY LIKE THE STRAY CATS ANYMORE.
ME NEITHER.
...EVERYTHING WOULD CHANGE AGAIN.

WAS I THE ONLY ONE WHO WASN'T SURE WHAT WAS COOL AND WHAT WASN'T?

DID ANYONE ELSE NOTICE THAT CASEY'S DAD'S CAR LOOKS LIKE KERMIT THE FROG?

OH MY GOSH, YOU'RE RIGHT!
HAHA!
TOTALLY!

YEAH, HIS CAR IS ALL, RIBBIT! I'M KERMIT THE FROG!

YEAH, KIKI JUST SAID THAT.

RIGHT, I MEAN, UM...
I NEED TO REMEMBER THAT TAKING A JOKE TOO FAR ISN'T COOL.

BUT WHAT'S TOO FAR?

WHERE'S AMY?
DIDN'T YOU HEAR? SHE'S MAD AT ME FOR SOME REASON.

AT LEAST YOU'RE ALWAYS ON MY SIDE.
OF COURSE!

WAIT...AM I SUPPOSED TO BE MAD AT AMY NOW?

EVERYTHING WAS CONSTANTLY CHANGING.

I WAS NEVER SURE WHEN IT WAS OKAY TO BE SILLY...

I VANT TO SUCK YOUR BLOOD!
HAHA!

HA-HA-HA-HA-HA-HA!!!

DO YOU...UM...WANNA GO PLAY?
I DUNNO. I GUESS NOT.
...OR WHEN WE WERE SUPPOSED TO BE MATURE.

WHEEEEEE!
HAHAHAHA!

WHAT DO YOU GUYS WANT TO DO?

I KNOW! LET'S SAY WE'RE IN A PRIVATE HELICOPTER ON OUR WAY TO PARIS.

I THOUGHT THE GAMES I MADE UP WERE WHAT MADE MY FRIENDS LIKE ME.
SUCH ROUGH AIR! I DO HOPE WE DON'T CRASH!
YES, I HOPE WE GET THERE IN TIME FOR THE PRIVATE YACHT PARTY.

WAIT, WHO AM I SUPPOSED TO BE?
YOU AND AMY ARE SISTERS. JEN AND I ARE SISTERS. AND WE'RE ALL COUSINS.
AND SUPER RICH, RIGHT?
YUP.

AAAAAAHH!!!

UUHH...
OHHH...

WHAT A HORRIBLE HELICOPTER CRASH ONTO THIS TROPICAL ISLAND. IS EVERYBODY OKAY?

AAAAAAAAAH!

YEAH, THAT WAS A HORRIBLE CRASH.
I THINK MY ARM IS BROKEN.
OOH, YEAH, INJURIES ARE GOOD.

OH NO, THE PILOT IS DEAD! AND HE HAD FIFTEEN CHILDREN!

WHAT DO WE DO NOW?
SOMETHING IS WASHING ONTO THE BEACH!
WAIT, WE'RE ON A BEACH?

MAYBE IT WILL GIVE US A CLUE AS TO WHERE WE ARE...

...AND WHAT CAUSED THAT CRASH.

LOOK, SISTER, THE SEA HAS GIVEN US A GIFT. IT APPEARS TO BE AN ANCIENT TREASURE!

SHANNON? I DON'T REALLY WANT TO PLAY THIS RIGHT NOW.

OH! UM...OKAY.

HEY.

HEY.

WHERE ARE YOU GUYS GOING?
TABLE SUPPLY.

WE SHOULD GO TO TABLE SUPPLY TOO.
I HAVE A QUARTER. THAT'LL BUY TWENTY-FIVE GUMMY BERRIES!

JEN, DO YOU LIKE RED OR PURPLE GUMMY BERRIES BEST?
RED. ALWAYS RED.

ARE YOU SAD THAT WE'RE NOT PLAYING YOUR GAME ANYMORE?
WHAT?

NO, NO, IT'S TOTALLY FINE.

IN SIXTH GRADE, IT SEEMED LIKE WE HAD TO PLAY A DIFFERENT KIND OF PRETEND.

DID YOU GUYS SEE A-TEAM ON THURSDAY?
I LAUGHED SO HARD WHEN MURDOCK SAID, "HANG ON, I WANT TO TRY SOMETHING I SAW IN A CARTOON ONCE."

The waves rushed against Alexandra's ankles,
but they couldn't wash away her sadness.

Alexandra sighed. Some girls would give anything to be the daughter of a multimillionaire.

What wouldn't she give to have normal parents and go to normal school.

It was so lonely being an only child, no sisters to talk to.

And now that she was home for the summer, her boarding school friends were far away.

"Never mind all that, I'm going to be just fine," said Alexandra,
because she was a brave girl with great potential and never stayed sad for long.

Something glittered knowingly
under a sudden rush of waves.

Then the waves pulled back,

giving Alexandra the gift.

It was a beautiful emerald,
swinging on a gold chain.

"Perhaps it's an ancient treasure," said Alexandra.

She slipped it over her head and gazed out into the ocean, saying thank you for the gift.
Although she did not see it, for a moment the stone glowed with the powerful magic it held inside...
...and the tips of her hair began to turn to flames, showing the great power she had and her true goodness.

HEY SHANNON.
HI JENNY.

AFTER YEARS OF MEANNESS...
I LIKED YOUR AUTUMN POEM.
REALLY?

THANKS!
...JENNY'S KINDNESS FELT LIKE FIREWORKS.

CYNTHIA! AMANDA!

SO, HEY, YOU WANNA COME OVER TO MY HOUSE?
SURE! BUT I HAVE TO WALK MY SISTER AND HER FRIEND HOME FIRST.

REMEMBER IN FOURTH GRADE WHEN THAT MAGICIAN DID AN ASSEMBLY?
OH MY HECK, THAT WAS HILARIOUS!

AM I FINALLY, FINALLY BECOMING REAL FRIENDS WITH JENNY???

HELLO!

HI AMANDA! DID YOU HAVE A GOOD DAY?

THANKS, SHANNON.
THANK YOU!

HER MOM PAYS YOU TO WALK HER HOME?
YEP! SHE HIRED ME FOR THE WHOLE YEAR.

JENNY AND I HAD A PRETTY GOOD TIME.
EVERYBODY WANTS TO RULE THE WORLD

YOU CAN GO HOME NOW.
UM...OKAY.
NOT PERFECT, BUT PRETTY GOOD.

BRIIIING!!!

MRS. GRANGER? HAVE YOU SEEN MY GLASSES?
YOU WOULDN'T LOSE THEM IF YOU DIDN'T KEEP TAKING THEM OFF ALL THE TIME.

I NEED TO GET GOING.
OKAY...

CYNTHIA!!

WHERE'S AMANDA?
I DON'T KNOW.

AMANDA!
AMANDA!

AMANDA?

SOMETIMES I FELT LIKE THIS JUST OUT OF NOWHERE—POUNDING HEART, SHORT OF BREATH.

WHAT'S THE MATTER?
I CAN'T BREATHE.
I DON'T THINK THERE'S ENOUGH AIR.
MY MOM TOOK ME TO A DOCTOR ONCE TO SEE IF I HAD ASTHMA OR SOMETHING, BUT THEY SAID I WAS FINE.

AMANDA! YOU'RE OKAY!

A DIFFERENT GIRL WALKED HER HOME. JENNY.
JENNY?
JENNY SAID AMANDA WAS JUST WAITING BY HERSELF. SHE SAID YOU NEVER SHOWED UP.

I WAS LATE, BUT I WAS COMING. I WOULD'VE GOTTEN HER.
I'M SORRY THIS HAPPENED, LINDA. SHANNON WAS SO WORRIED. SHE SEARCHED THE ENTIRE SCHOOL.

WELL, I PAID JENNY THIS TIME.
SHE OFFERED TO WALK HER HOME EVERY DAY.

PLEASE! I CAN STILL DO IT.

WE'LL SEE.

LET'S GO TALK TO JENNY.

NO! NOT NOW! SHE'LL MAKE FUN OF ME FOR CRYING!

I WANTED TO PREPARE.
I NEEDED TO THINK IT THROUGH.

WHAT SHOULD I DO?

JENNY HAD TO KNOW I'D FIND OUT IT WAS HER.

SHE'S THE SAME OLD JENNY.

THINKS SHE CAN DO ANYTHING SHE WANTS TO ME AND THERE'S NOTHING I CAN DO ABOUT IT.

WHAT IF SHE LIES TO JEN ABOUT WHAT HAPPENED?

MAYBE SHE'S THE ONE WHO SAID BAD THINGS ABOUT ME TO NICOLE AND AMY.

HI, IS JENNY HERE?
SHE'LL BE BACK SOON. WHY DON'T YOU COME ON IN?

TICK TICK TICK

YOU'VE ALWAYS BEEN SO NICE AND THIN.

THANKS...

GROWN-UPS WERE ALWAYS WEIRDLY EXCITED ABOUT SKINNINESS.

YOUR DAUGHTER IS SO THIN! ISN'T SHE LUCKY?
SLIM FAST

BUT TO OTHER KIDS...
LOOK! I ALMOST FIT GRANDMA'S DRESS!
HAHA! YOU LOOK LIKE A BLUE TOOTHPICK!

HEY BEANPOLE.

WOW, HER ARMS ARE LIKE STICKS.
CAREFUL, HER ELBOWS CAN DRAW BLOOD.

SAY CHEESE!
HURRY, SHANNON HAS A BONY BUTT!

WHETHER PEOPLE WERE TRYING TO BE NICE OR MEAN...

...IT ALWAYS FELT WEIRD WHEN SOMEONE TALKED ABOUT MY BODY.
YES, JENNY IS FINALLY THINNING OUT.

IT TAKES LONGER FOR SOME GIRLS TO LOSE THEIR BABY FAT. YOU'RE SO LUCKY YOU'VE ALWAYS BEEN THIN!
I GUESS...

HERE SHE IS!

JENNY, SHANNON CAME TO SEE YOU.

TICK TICK TICK

JENNY, IT'S MY RESPONSIBILITY TO WALK AMANDA HOME. YOU SHOULDN'T HAVE TAKEN HER.

WELL, YOU WEREN'T AROUND.

I WAS IN THE CLASSROOM. YOU KNEW I WALK HER HOME. IT'S LIKE YOU TRIED TO STEAL MY JOB TO GET THE MONEY.

NO, I WAS WORRIED ABOUT HER!

THEN YOU COULD HAVE LOOKED FOR ME OR WAITED WITH HER TILL I GOT THERE.

WELL...
PLEASE DON'T DO THAT AGAIN.

OKAY.

MY BIG SISTER WENDY WAS LIVING IN LOS ANGELES, TRYING TO BECOME A MODEL.
HOW'S THE SITUATION WITH THE JENNIFERS?
WHEN I ASKED JEN IF WE WERE BEST FRIENDS, SHE SAID YES!

BUT, UM...

UM...

I TALKED TO JENNY ABOUT STEALING AMANDA FROM ME. IT WENT OKAY. BUT I STILL FEEL LIKE SHE HATES ME.

SHE'S INSECURE. SHE DOESN'T LIKE HERSELF, SO SHE NEEDS TO MAKE YOU FEEL BAD TOO.

I DON'T KNOW ABOUT THAT...
TRUST ME. BULLIES USUALLY HATE THEMSELVES THE MOST.

FOR YEARS, JENNY AND JEN HAD BEEN BEST FRIENDS.

HEY SHANNON! DID YOU CALL YOUR SISTER LAST NIGHT?
BUT JEN AND I WERE BEST FRIENDS NOW.

I LOVED BEING CLOSE TO JEN AND FEELING LIKE I WAS ON TOP. BUT HOW TO STAY THERE?
YEAH, AND GUESS WHO SHE SAW WALKING DOWN HOLLYWOOD BOULEVARD?
WHO?

MICHAEL J. FOX!

EEEEEE!!!
*THE A-TEAM* WAS SO GOOD LAST NIGHT.

OH MY GOSH YES!

MR. T IS SO FUNNY.
SHANNON, DID YOU FIGURE OUT THE MYSTERY BEFORE THE END?
UM, NO, I DIDN'T WATCH *THE A-TEAM* YESTERDAY.

WHAT ABOUT *SIMON & SIMON*?
NO, NOT THAT EITHER.
MY PARENTS DIDN'T LIKE US WATCHING TV ON SCHOOL NIGHTS.

AND WE DIDN'T HAVE ANY WAY TO RECORD SHOWS.
A.J. IS MY FAVORITE.
YEAH, A.J. IS SO FINE!
I LIKE RICK BETTER.

WHAT? RICK HAS A MUSTACHE!
GROSS!
I DON'T WANT TO KISS HIM! I JUST THINK HE'S FUNNY!
BUT I WASN'T GOING TO BE LEFT OUT, NOT IN SIXTH GRADE.

I HAVE TO WATCH *THE A-TEAM* AND *SIMON & SIMON*, MOM! ALL MY FRIENDS DO!
YOU KNOW THE RULES. EVENING IS HOMEWORK TIME.

BUT IT IS HOMEWORK. HOMEWORK FOR RECESS CLASS.
ON FRIDAYS AT RECESS, THAT'S ALL ANYONE TALKS ABOUT.

I GET LEFT OUT WHEN I DON'T KNOW WHAT THEY'RE TALKING ABOUT. I'M AFRAID I'LL LOSE ALL MY FRIENDS.

PLUS I'VE ALREADY DONE ALL MY OTHER HOMEWORK. PLEASE, MOM? PLEASE?

WHAT DO YOU THINK YOU'RE DOING?
HOMEWORK.

MOM! SHANNON'S ALWAYS WATCHING TV!

*SIMON & SIMON* WAS SO GOOD LAST NIGHT.

I LOVED THE CHIMP! IT WAS SO FUNNY!

I KNOW. I ALWAYS WANTED A PET CHIMP.

DO YOU WANT TO GO TRICK-OR-TREATING TOGETHER THIS YEAR?
SURE. JENNY ASKED ME TO GO WITH HER, BUT I SAID I HAD TAKE MY NIECE AROUND.

DON'T TELL HER.
OKAY.

JEN LIED TO GET OUT
OF BEING WITH JENNY.

BUT SHE WANTS
TO BE WITH ME.
WE REALLY ARE BEST FRIENDS!

I THINK THAT'S JENNY OVER THERE.

WHERE?
I HAD TO SQUINT TO SEE ANYTHING FAR AWAY. I NEVER FOUND MY LOST GLASSES.

COME ON!
I USED TO HIDE IN THE PLAYGROUND SHRUBS WHEN JENNY WAS MEAN TO ME.

BUT THIS WAS GOOD SHRUB HIDING.
MOSTLY GOOD. I FELT A LITTLE BAD.

BUT I ALSO FELT A LITTLE AMAZING.

FINALLY, I WASN'T THE ONE BEING LEFT OUT.

FLUSH

OH, HEY NICOLE.

HEY, NOT TO BE RUDE
OR ANYTHING...

BUT JEN TOLD ME SHE
DOESN'T LIKE YOU.

WHAT?
NOT TO BE RUDE.
JUST THOUGHT YOU'D
WANNA KNOW.

SIXTH-GRADE FRIENDSHIPS WERE LIKE A GAME...

ONLY AS SOON AS I'D FIGURE OUT THE RULES...
...THEY'D CHANGE AGAIN.
NEW RULES
NEWEST RULES


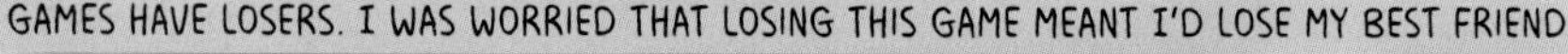

GAMES HAVE LOSERS. I WAS WORRIED THAT LOSING THIS GAME MEANT I'D LOSE MY BEST FRIEND.

SHANNON?
COMING.

IF JEN SAID SHE DIDN'T LIKE ME, MAYBE IT'S BECAUSE JENNY IS TELLING HER LIES ABOUT ME AGAIN?
SO SHE CAN GO BACK TO BEING HER BEST FRIEND?
I FIGURED I'D HAVE TO TELL JEN BAD STUFF ABOUT JENNY.

SO, JENNY LIES A LOT.

YEAH, I KNOW.
I KNEW IT WAS BAD TO GOSSIP.

BUT JUST THEN, GOSSIP FELT LIKE SURVIVAL.
SHE USED TO TELL YOU LIES ABOUT ME.

TO MAKE YOU HATE ME.
OH MY GOSH.

WHEN?
A MILLION TIMES.
LIKE, WHAT DID SHE SAY?
IT WAS SUCH A RELIEF TO TELL JEN AT LAST.

NOW I WAS THE ONE TALKING BEHIND JENNY'S BACK.
I FELT POWERFUL.

WHEN I WAS IN FIFTH GRADE, ALL THE SIXTH GRADERS HAD SEEMED SO GROWN-UP. LIKE THEY KNEW EVERYTHING.
I KEPT WAITING TO FEEL LIKE I KNEW EVERYTHING.

I HEARD YOU SAID I'M A LIAR.

WHAT?
ARE YOU GOSSIPING ABOUT ME?

GOSSIPING IS A SIN.

I'M...I'M SORRY.

I KNEW SHE WAS WAITING FOR ME TO CRY AND RUN AWAY SO SHE COULD CALL ME A BABY.

FOR ONCE, I STOPPED MYSELF FROM CRYING!

STILL, ALL THOSE FEELINGS HAD TO GO SOMEWHERE.
THE CASE OF THE TELLTALE CHIN
HEY SHANNON, AREN'T YOU GOING TO CRY?

HER EYES WERE DRY.

HER VOICE WAS CALM.

BUT THE QUIVER IN HER CHIN GAVE HER AWAY!

MAJOR CHIN-QUIVERING ACTION

JENNY HAD BULLIED ME FOR YEARS.

I WASN'T LETTING HER GET AWAY WITH IT ANYMORE!
WHEN I WAS AT YOUR HOUSE THE OTHER DAY, YOUR MOM SAID YOU'RE FINALLY THINNING OUT.

WHAT ARE YOU TALKING ABOUT?

YOUR MOM. SHE SAID SOME GIRLS TAKE LONGER TO LOSE THEIR BABY FAT BUT THAT YOU FINALLY WERE.

UM...

I WAS SHAKING.
I FELT A LITTLE SICK.
BUT I ALSO FELT A LITTLE...

...AMAZING.
HOW CAN DOING SOMETHING FEEL BOTH GOOD AND BAD AT THE SAME TIME?

THE AMAZING FEELING WENT AWAY PRETTY QUICKLY, JUST LEAVING THE SICK FEELING.

THE NEXT DAY.
SHANNON!

I ASKED MY MOM, AND SHE NEVER SAID THAT.
WHAT?

SHE NEVER SAID ANY OF THAT! YOU'RE A LIAR.

I AM NOT!

SHE DID TOO SAY IT. SHE DID!

YOU ARE A LIAR. YOU ARE MEAN.

AND EVERYONE THINKS RED HAIR IS WEIRD.

I KNEW I DIDN'T MAKE IT UP.
BUT I ALSO KNEW I NEVER SHOULD HAVE REPEATED IT.

HEAVENLY FATHER, PLEASE PLEASE PLEASE FORGIVE ME.

I DON'T WANT TO BE MEAN, I DON'T KNOW WHAT TO DO...

ALL THOSE TIMES THAT JENNY SAID MEAN THINGS TO ME...

...ALL THOSE TIMES SHE TOLD PEOPLE STUFF ABOUT ME BEHIND MY BACK...

...DID SHE FEEL BAD ABOUT IT AFTER? DID IT GIVE HER STOMACHACHES TOO?

I CAN'T GO TO SCHOOL TODAY. I'M SICK. MY STOMACH HURTS.
AGAIN? BUT YOU'VE BEEN DOING SO MUCH BETTER THIS YEAR.

IT'S NOT IN MY HEAD, MOM! I REALLY DO FEEL SICK!
OKAY, OKAY.

BRIINNNNG!

SIXTH GRADE WAS BETTER THAN BEFORE...

HEY SHANNON, WHERE WERE YOU YESTERDAY?
OH...I WAS SICK.

I'M GLAD YOU'RE FEELING BETTER!

...BUT IT WAS STILL HARD SOMETIMES.

I'm sorry. Do you forgive me?
no
yes

Although Alexandra was smart and fun, she wasn't always sure if her friends at boarding school were really her friends.

"At least at boarding school, I wasn't alone," Alexandra said to herself. "Not like home. Just me and my tears to keep me company."

Even though Alexandra was only home for one month every year, her parents had left her for a Caribbean vacation.

"Well," said Alexandra, "if Mother and Father can go to a tropical island, so can I. At least, in a way."

Her favorite room in the manor had glass walls and contained many beautiful tropical plants and trees, chimpanzees, black panthers...

...and her favorite cat...

...Shasta the lion.
That night, Alexandra fell asleep in the jungle room...
...and woke up in a real jungle.

"Excuse me," said Alexandra,
"can you tell me where we are?"

"She has the fire hair," said the peasant man.
"The law says we must capture her and take her to Drithvan!"

Usually Shasta's big, brown eyes showed love for Alexandra, but when there was danger, his eyes changed to a fierce red.

"Shasta," said Alexandra,

"I think we're a long way from my father's safe, two million-dollar mansion."

# Chapter Two

Do you like someone?

Check one!

☐ YES!

☐ NO

☐ I'm not telling

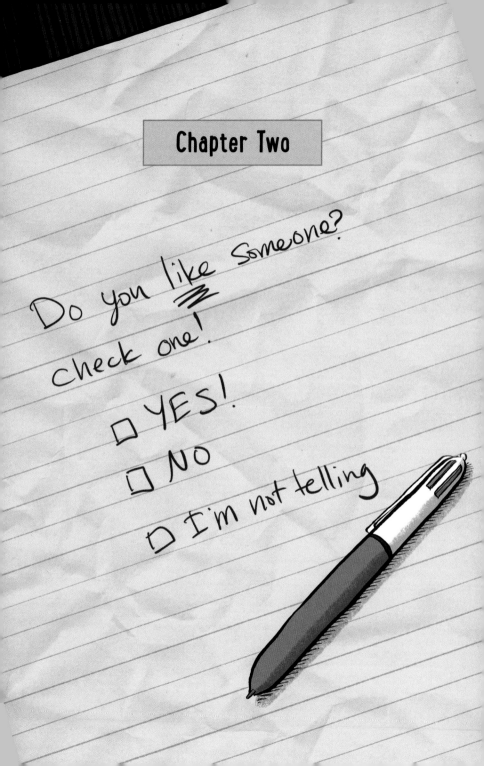

IN PRESCHOOL, ONE OF MY BEST FRIENDS WAS A BOY.

I WAS A KID, HE WAS A KID, SO WE WERE FRIENDS. NO BIG DEAL.

BUT IN KINDERGARTEN, THERE SEEMED TO BE NEW RULES ABOUT BOYS AND GIRLS.

...AND SHE WAS PLAYING HOUSE WITH JIMMY...

RULE: GIRLS AND BOYS AREN'T SUPPOSED TO PLAY TOGETHER?

BIG, SCARY BOYS.

SMACK!!

WATCH OUT, CRYBABY.

KINDERGARTEN BABY, BORN IN THE GRAVY!

BORN IN THE GRAVY? WHAT THE HECK DOES THAT MEAN?

HERE.

OOH! YOU GOT GIRL COOTIES ON THE BALL!

SO...YOU'RE SCARED OF ME?

AAAARRRR

AAAAAHHHH!

MWAH!

MAH!
GROSS!
HELP!!

GAAARR!!!

EEEEE!!!

AAAHHHH!!!

HOW WAS YOUR DAY?
GOOD. ADRIENNE AND I PLAYED WITH SOME BOYS AT RECESS.
THAT'S GREAT!

YEAH! 'CAUSE THEY WERE SCARED OF ME! IT WAS SO FUN!
SCARED OF YOU?

WELL...BOYS LIKE GIRLS WHO ARE SHY.
SHY?

MM-HM. BEING SHY AND QUIET IS THE BEST WAY TO GET BOYS TO LIKE YOU. THAT'S WHAT MY MOTHER TAUGHT ME.

RULE: GIRLS ARE SUPPOSED TO GET BOYS TO LIKE THEM FOR SOME REASON? AND BE SHY TOO???

MWAH!
AAAH!

MWAH!
EEEE!!!

HI.
BUT I JUST COULDN'T BE SHY.

EEEEEK!!!

GOT YOU!
OH NO! I'M POISONED!

STOP!!!

THERE WILL BE NO MORE KISSING GAMES.
THAT SPREADS GERMS.

I WILL CALL YOUR PARENTS
IF YOU DO IT AGAIN.

RULE: GIRLS KISSING BOYS IS BAD?

I MISS OUR GAME.

YEAH, ME TOO.

COME ON, GIRLS ARE GROSS.

YEAH, GIRLS ARE GROSS.

NO WE'RE NOT!
WHY DO THEY SAY THAT?
THAT'S JUST WHAT BOYS THINK.

GIRLS ARE SUPPOSED TO GET BOYS TO LIKE THEM. BUT BOYS ARE SUPPOSED TO THINK GIRLS ARE GROSS?

BY SECOND GRADE, I'D FIGURED OUT A NEW RULE...
WHO DO YOU LIKE IN OUR CLASS?
UM...JUSTIN.

...GIRLS WEREN'T ALLOWED TO LIKE BOYS UNLESS WE LIKE-LIKED THEM.

FOR THE HOLIDAY ASSEMBLY, WE'LL BE DOING A FOLK DANCE!

TO PAIR YOU UP, I'M GOING TO HAVE EACH BOY PICK A GIRL.

I PICK...UM, JENNI M.

I PICK JENNIFER S.

I PICK JENNY G.

NEXT UP IS JUSTIN.

GO AHEAD AND PICK A GIRL.
I PICK...

ADRIENNE.

AND LAST IS GAVIN, SO YOU'LL BE PAIRED WITH SHANNON.

HEY SHANNON, YOU MUST BE HEARTBROKEN.
YEAH, WE HEARD YOU LIKE JUSTIN...
NO, I DON'T!

RULE: GIRLS ARE SUPPOSED TO LIKE-LIKE BOYS, BUT IT'S EMBARRASSING IF WE'RE CAUGHT LIKE-LIKING THEM.

IN THIRD GRADE CAME...
...THE GROUP.

THERE WAS A GROUP OF POPULAR BOYS TOO, BUT THEY DIDN'T HAVE A LEADER LIKE JEN.

RULE: GIRLS IN THE GROUP ARE ONLY ALLOWED TO LIKE THE GROUP OF POPULAR BOYS.

SNARF!!
SNURF!!
SNARF!!

THEN IN SIXTH GRADE, ALL THE RULES STARTED TO CHANGE.

WHOA, YOUR FINGERNAILS ARE FREAKY LONG.

YEAH, WATCH OUT.

I'M THE CLAW AND I'LL GET YOU!

BEWARE THE CLAW!
LET'S GET THEM!
HA!

RULE: IN SIXTH GRADE, IT'S OKAY TO BE FRIENDS WITH BOYS AGAIN?

MAYBE?

HAVE YOU TRIED SOUR PATCH KIDS YET?
I ATE AN ENTIRE HANDFUL ONCE. SO SOUR!
BRRRIIIINNNNGGGG!!!

ARR!!
I AM THE MIGHTY SNARF!

KLONK!!

BRANDON?
ARE YOU OKAY?
UHHH...

I'LL GET HELP!

OH MY GOSH.
DO YOU THINK HE'LL BE OKAY?
I DIDN'T MEAN TO...

THE REST OF THE DAY FELT LIKE IT LASTED FOREVER.

I CALLED HIS MOM.

BRANDON GOT A CONCUSSION.
OH NO.
WE SHOULD DO SOMETHING.

OKAY, WE'VE GOT...
Table
Table Supply

...$2.78 ALTOGETHER.

MY MOM TOOK CYNTHIA AND AMANDA HOME SO I COULD GO WITH EVERYONE TO VISIT BRANDON.

YES?
UM...

I'M REALLY SORRY. I'M THE ONE WHO HURT BRANDON.

IT WAS AN ACCIDENT.
WE BROUGHT TREATS.

CAN WE GIVE THEM TO BRANDON?

BRANDON, YOU HAVE VISITORS.

MOM!!

SLAM!!!

HEY BRANDON.
ARE YOU OKAY?
DUDE, I'M REALLY SORRY.
IT'S OKAY.

I'D NEVER BEEN IN A BOY'S ROOM BEFORE.
GOONIES

HEY, YOU HAVE OINGO BOINGO.

IT'S A DEAD MAN'S PARTY...

AND ANOTHER RULE CHANGE—NOW IT'S OKAY FOR GIRLS TO HANG OUT WITH BOYS AFTER SCHOOL?

"Shasta, you stay here and hide in the jungle," said Alexandra. "I'll try to find out what's going on."

In this strange place, her red hair made people afraid for some reason.

"Excuse me," said Alexandra, "I'm lost. Can you tell me where we are?"

"Why, this is Cambernath," said the fruit vendor, "a market town in the great kingdom of Drithvan . . .

...may Drithvan rule in fear forever."

"Too much chatting," said a soldier. "No conversations, by order of Drithvan."

"I was just asking a question," Alexandra said.

But the soldier shoved her so hard she probably had a bruise.

"Hey now," said a peasant boy, "no reason to hurt the girl."

Alexandra rushed to the peasant boy to see if he was okay.

She didn't realize that her hood fell off, revealing her fire-red hair.

When the soldier saw her red hair, he shouted out with real alarm.

And then he raised his sword like he was going to cut off her head.

But the peasant boys pulled Alexandra away before she could get her head chopped off.

"Shasta!" Alexandra called out. "Help us!"

Shasta's mighty roar shook the jungle.

He raised his dangerous claws. The soldiers fled in terror.

As they walked through the jungle, they talked like regular kids who had been friends for years. And even though Alexandra was a girl and they were boys...
...there was nothing weird about it at all.

SOMETIMES IT SEEMED LIKE BOYS DIDN'T WORRY ABOUT THE RULES. MAYBE THINGS WERE EASIER FOR THEM.

LOOK OUT, IT'S SHAWN!
SHEEPY SHAWN.

SHTUPID SHAWN.
OR EASIER FOR SOME OF THEM ANYWAY.

I DIDN'T KNOW WHY NO ONE LIKED SHAWN.

MAYBE IT STARTED IN THIRD GRADE WHEN HIS MOM CAME TO CLASS WEARING SO MUCH PERFUME.
SHE BROUGHT HIS BIRTHDAY TREAT, BUT INSTEAD OF THE USUAL HOMEMADE CUPCAKES...
...IT WAS A BAG OF CANDY. COFFEE-FLAVORED CANDY.

A BUNCH OF US WEREN'T ALLOWED TO DRINK COFFEE, SO WE GAVE OUR CANDY BACK.
AND SHE YELLED AT US.

WHAT'S THE MATTER WITH YOU KIDS? IT'S JUST CANDY!!!

MAYBE THAT'S WHY NO ONE LIKED HIM.

OR WHY HE DIDN'T LIKE US.

YOU'RE ALL NERDS.

UH, YEAH, SHAWN, WE'RE THE NERDS.
HAHA!

JESUS WOULD WANT ME TO STAND UP FOR HIM.
I SHOULD SAY SOMETHING.

BUT I DIDN'T. I WAS TOO SCARED. THE WAY EVERYONE TREATED SHAWN...
THAT'S WHAT COULD HAPPEN TO ME TOO.

IF I LOST JEN AS MY BEST FRIEND.

BUT I FELT BAD FOR SHAWN, SO I MADE A PLAN TO GIVE HIM A LETTER IN HIS VALENTINE'S BOX ON VALENTINE'S DAY.

Dear Shawn,
I don't like how everyone treats you. It's not nice. I wish people would be nicer.

I HAD IT READY TO GO A WHOLE MONTH IN ADVANCE.

BUT THEN...
LET'S TAKE A VOTE. RAISE YOUR HAND IF YOU'RE TOO OLD TO DO VALENTINES THIS YEAR?

NO! BUT...SHAWN'S LETTER!

BUT ALSO...THEY'RE VOTING TO NOT GET CANDY? WHAT'S THE MATTER WITH THEM?

ALL RIGHT, THEN, NO VALENTINES THIS YEAR.
FINALLY. PASSING OUT VALENTINES IS SO BABYISH.

YEAH...

OKAY, CLASS, FOR TODAY'S JOURNAL ENTRY, WRITE ABOUT WHAT YOU WANT TO BE WHEN YOU GROW UP.

BOYS WERE LUCKY. IT SEEMED LIKE THEY COULD BE ANYTHING THEY WANTED.

ALL THE WOMEN I KNEW WERE EITHER MOMS OR TEACHERS. BUT WHAT IF...

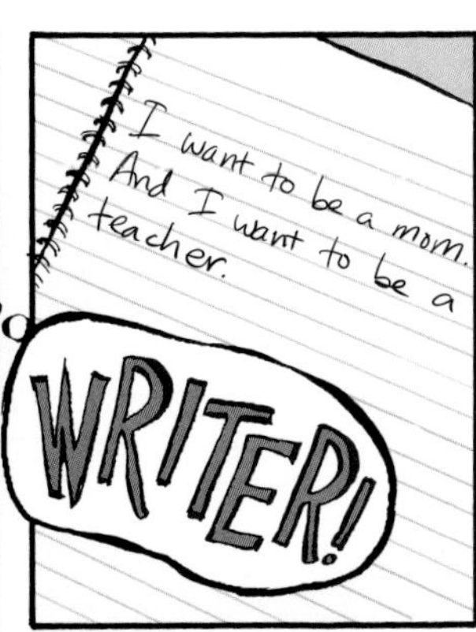
I want to be a mom.
And I want to be a teacher.
WRITER!

I'D NEVER MET A WRITER. IT DIDN'T SEEM POSSIBLE FOR ME.

HOW MANY OF YOU WROTE...
NASA
14 DAYS
CHRISTA McAULIFFE

...ASTRONAUT?
NASA
14 DAYS
CHRISTA McAULIFFE

AS A FOLLOW-UP, WRITE ABOUT SOMEONE YOU KNOW WHO YOU THINK SHOULD BE THE NEXT CIVILIAN ASTRONAUT.

FOR THE FIRST TIME EVER, A REGULAR PERSON WAS GOING INTO SPACE—AND NOT JUST ANYONE.
A WOMAN.
CHRISTA MCAULIFFE.

CHRISTA MCAULIFFE WAS A MOM AND A TEACHER. BUT NOW SHE WAS ALSO AN ASTRONAUT.

NASA
NASA

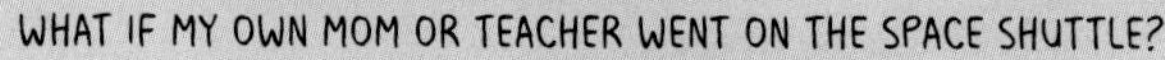
WHAT IF MY OWN MOM OR TEACHER WENT ON THE SPACE SHUTTLE?

OR A GIRL LIKE ME?

NASA
MAYBE THE RULES WERE CHANGING FOR GIRLS. LIKE CHRISTA MCAULIFFE, MAYBE WE COULD BE MORE THAN WHAT WE'D THOUGHT WAS POSSIBLE.

EVER SINCE OUR PARTY AT BRANDON'S, JEN AND JUSTIN WERE "GOING TOGETHER."

"GOING TOGETHER" MEANT THAT THEY LIKE-LIKED EACH OTHER. BUT, OFFICIALLY.

SHANNON!

EYES ON YOUR OWN WORK.

AFTER JEN AND JUSTIN, LOTS OF OUR FRIENDS STARTED GOING WITH BOYS FROM THE BOYS' GROUP.

THEY "WENT TOGETHER."
KIKI
AARON

BY SIXTH GRADE, I'D SPENT A LOT OF YEARS TRYING TO FIGURE OUT HOW A GIRL WAS SUPPOSED TO BE.

SOMEDAY WHEN YOU'RE TAKING CARE OF YOUR HUSBAND...

DAD

A WOMAN'S FIRST MOST IMPORTANT JOB IS BEING A WIFE...

CHURCH

THE MOMENT I SAW HER I FELL IN LOVE. HER BEAUTIFUL FACE IS ALL I'M THINKING OF...

RADIO

PLEASE, GREG, TAKE ME BACK! I'M NOTHING WITHOUT YOU!

T.V.

MOM

BOYS LIKE GIRLS WHO ARE...

1. THE MOST IMPORTANT THING FOR A GIRL IS TO GROW UP AND GET MARRIED.

2. I WON'T BE ABLE TO GET MARRIED UNLESS BOYS LIKE ME.

3. IF BOYS DON'T LIKE ME, THEN I'M NOT IMPORTANT.

4. IN ORDER TO GET BOYS TO LIKE ME, I HAVE TO BE... BEAUTIFUL?

5. SO, THE MOST IMPORTANT THING FOR A GIRL IS TO BE BEAUTIFUL.

Seventeen

THIS IS TAKING FOREVER.

GOOD THING WE DON'T HAVE TO MAKE A CURSED PYRAMID THEN.
'CAUSE THAT WOULD TAKE EVEN LONGER.

A BUMMER THAT MY MOM COULDN'T FIND ANY CURSED SUGAR CUBES AT THE STORE.
AND MAKING OUR OWN CURSE IS SO TIME-CONSUMING. AND MESSY.

YEAH, AND WHERE ARE WE GOING TO FIND AN ARMADILLO KING TO SACRIFICE AT THIS HOUR?

HA!

MY MOM'S BEEN DATING THAT GUY FROM CALIFORNIA FOR, LIKE, MONTHS, AND SHE DIDN'T EVEN TELL US...

HI DANIEL.

POSSIBLE RULE: IF A BOY LOOKS AT YOU A LOT, THAT MIGHT MEAN HE LIKES YOU?

UTAH
Friday Read-A-Thon

NEW RULE: IF A BOY PUTS HIS HEAD ON YOUR PILLOW, DOES THAT MEAN HE LIKES YOU?

WE'D BEEN MAKING "RATING CALLS" TO THE BOYS IN OUR CLASS SINCE THIRD GRADE, ASKING THEM TO RATE OUR "LOOKS" AND "PERSONALITY."

BUT IN SIXTH GRADE, WE ADDED A NEW CATEGORY.
WHAT DO YOU RATE JEN ON LOOKS, PERSONALITY, AND BODY?

I'D NEVER REALIZED BEFORE THAT THE BOYS MIGHT BE LOOKING AT OUR BODIES.
Personality
Face
Body
Shannon
6
5
4
Jen
10
10
10
WAS THERE A CERTAIN WAY WE WERE SUPPOSED TO LOOK?

I THOUGHT GIRLS WERE SUPPOSED TO WANT BOYS TO LIKE US. BUT IT WAS WEIRD TO THINK THEY MIGHT WANT TO LOOK AT US.

TO LOOK AT OUR BODIES.

WHO SHOULD WE CALL NEXT?
UM...HOW ABOUT DANIEL?

WHY?
I DON'T KNOW. JUST 'CAUSE.

DANIEL WASN'T IN THE POPULAR BOYS' GROUP. BUT I WONDERED IF THAT REALLY MATTERED?

HI, IS DANIEL THERE?

HI, THIS IS A RATING CALL.
OKAY.

WHAT DO YOU RATE...JEN, ON FACE, BODY, AND PERSONALITY?

EIGHT, EIGHT, AND EIGHT.

NOW HOW ABOUT SHANNON?

UM...SEVEN AND A HALF?
WELL, IT'S HIGHER THAN I USUALLY GET.

BUT IF A BOY LIKE-LIKES A GIRL, HE SHOULD RATE HER HIGHEST, SHOULDN'T HE?

WHY A HALF? HE COULDN'T EVEN ROUND UP?

BOYS WERE CONFUSING.

AND SOMETIMES...

VROOM!

SOMETIMES BOYS WERE SCARY.

HEY NICOLE! I'LL CALL YOU AS SOON AS I GET HOME, OKAY?

WHAT DID YOU SAY?

NOTHING!
NEVER MIND!

STILL, SEVEN AND A HALF WAS PRETTY GOOD?
MAYBE HE'D RATED ME LOWER THAN JEN JUST TO HIDE THAT HE LIKED ME...

OOPS.

SORRY.

OOPS.

SHANNON AND DANIEL, YOU CAN BOTH STAY IN FROM RECESS SINCE YOU CAN'T STOP PLAYING FOOTSIE.

OOOOOOHHH!!!!

SO HOW WAS FOOTSIE WITH SHANNON?
I WASN'T! I DIDN'T DO THAT!

DANIEL AND SHANNON, SITTIN' IN A—

I DON'T EVEN LIKE HER, OKAY? SHE'S A WEIRDO!

TIME TO GET UP.
MOM, I DON'T FEEL GOOD.
I DIDN'T WANT TO SEE DANIEL AGAIN SO SOON.

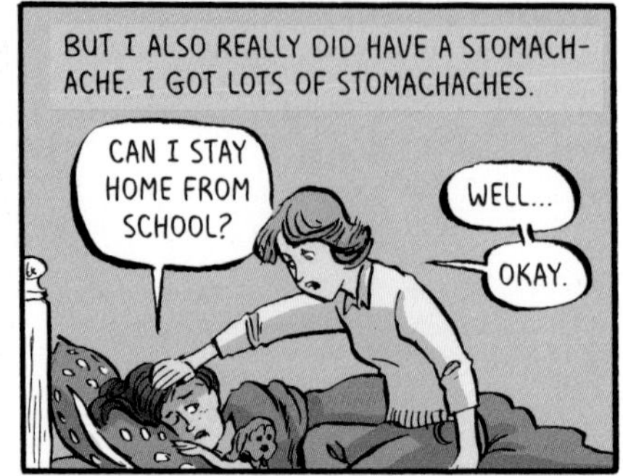
BUT I ALSO REALLY DID HAVE A STOMACH-ACHE. I GOT LOTS OF STOMACHACHES.
CAN I STAY HOME FROM SCHOOL?
WELL...
OKAY.

MOM, CAN I HAVE SOME—
...IT WAS AN UNUSUALLY COLD MORNING AT THE KENNEDY SPACE CENTER IN FLORIDA FOR THE *CHALLENGER*'S LAUNCH...

OH YEAH, THE *CHALLENGER* LAUNCH!
WE WERE GOING TO WATCH IT AT SCHOOL.

EVERY KID IN THE COUNTRY WAS WATCHING IT AT SCHOOL.
THEY JUST LAUNCHED, BUT SOMETHING WENT WRONG.

WE ARE STILL AWAITING CONFIRMATION...

...BUT SEVENTY SECONDS AFTER TAKEOFF...

...THE CRAFT APPEARED TO EXPLODE.

IT SEEMS LIKELY THAT ALL SEVEN CREW MEMBERS, INCLUDING TEACHER CHRISTA MCAULIFFE, DIDN'T SURVIVE THE EXPLOSION.
THAT'S TERRIBLE.

I FELT LIKE SOMEONE I KNEW HAD DIED.

SHE WAS A MOM. AND A TEACHER. AND SHE'D TRIED TO BE SOMETHING ELSE TOO.

MOM?

THE NEXT WEEK WHEN I RETURNED TO SCHOOL, I SAW DANIEL AGAIN.

BUT I WAS TIRED OF WONDERING ABOUT HIM.

BRANDON, AARON, EMILY, AND SHANNON, COME UP, PLEASE.
RIP
RIP

THE DISTRICT IS SENDING A SPECIAL TEACHER FOR AN ADVANCED LITERATURE GROUP. I'VE CHOSEN YOU FOUR TO BE A PART OF IT.

REALLY?

REALLY REALLY?
JUST...CALM DOWN, OKAY?

THIS IS MY FIRST TIME TEACHING CHILDREN. I'M EARNING MY PHD IN ENGLISH LITERATURE.
I'D NEVER MET A WOMAN WITH A PHD BEFORE.

GETTING A PHD WOULD BE SO COOL...

WE'RE GOING TO...UH...
...EXPLORE POETRY WITH...UM...
FLICK!

HEY, NOW.

STOP THAT, YOUNG MEN.

HER NAME WAS MISS HEPLER, AND WE THOUGHT SHE WAS A LITTLE ODD.

BUT WHEN SHE READ POETRY...
Now gold and purple SCINTILLATE/ On trees that seem dancing/ In delirium; Then the moon/ In a mad orange flare/ FLOODS the GRAPE-HUNG night...

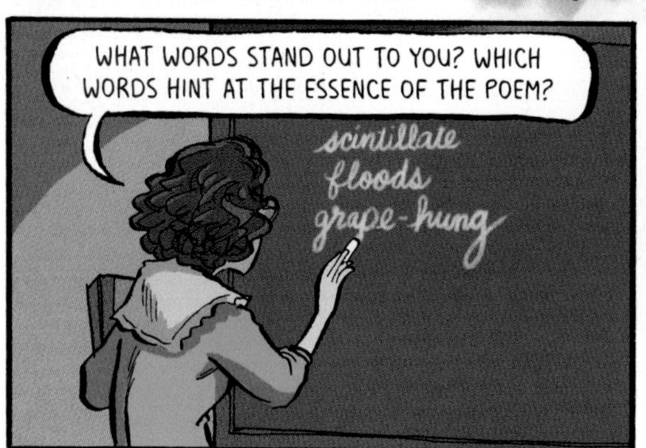
WHAT WORDS STAND OUT TO YOU? WHICH WORDS HINT AT THE ESSENCE OF THE POEM?
scintillate
floods
grape-hung

THE WHAT?

THE ESSENCE? THE...HEART OF IT. THE NITTY-GRITTY. WHAT A THING REALLY IS, DEEP DOWN, WHEN YOU CAN'T EXACTLY EXPLAIN IT.

WHAT IS YOUR ESSENCE? WHAT MAKES YOU WHO YOU ARE?
MY Essence? NO ONE'S EVER ASKED ME SOMETHING LIKE THAT BEFORE.

It was almost night, and the trees were dancing in a breeze.
The mad orange sun flooded the jungle with a final flare of fiery light.
"Thank you for saving me in the village," said Alexandra. "How can I ever repay you?"
"You can join our secret army," said the peasant boy. "We're all spies, and we're working in secret to defeat Drithvan."
Shasta was not comfortable around so many people, so he stayed in the jungle to hunt wild beasts.
A girl in fancy clothes explained that once upon a time, the good wizard Amerdath had ruled Athridor in peace. But the evil wizard Drithvan wanted their magic.

When Drithvan and his mighty army invaded, Amerdath stored all of Athridor's magic in the Emerald Star. He split the star into four pieces and scattered them into the sea to keep them safe.

"Emerald?" said Alexandra. "Could this green stone I found be part of the Emerald Star?"

Alexandra reached to the stone from the deepest part of her mind...

...and called back its ancient magic.

The magic lit up her essence, hidden there from the day of her birth. And the green stone of Amerdath awoke Alexandra's powers.

I LOOKED FORWARD TO OUR CLASS EVERY WEEK.
SOME OCEAN THROBBING FAR AND FREE WITH STORMS—BUT WHERE MEANWHILE...
ALL THE POETS WE READ WERE MEN WHO HAD BEEN DEAD A LONG TIME. IT MADE ME THINK THAT THE ONLY GOOD POETRY WAS OLD POETRY...

...SERENEST SKIES CONTINUALLY JUST O'ER THAT ONE BRIGHT ISLAND SMILE.

WHAT IS THE POEM'S ESSENCE?

LISTEN TO HOW THE POET TELLS YOU WHAT HE MEANS: "SOME OCEAN THROBBING FAR AND FREE..."

...AND THAT GIRLS COULDN'T BE POETS AT ALL.

THIS IS MY ESSENCE!

PBBB!!!

SIT DOWN, AARON.
PBBT! PBB

PBBBBT!
PBBBT!
SIT DOWN!
STOP IT!
IT FELT GOOD TO LAUGH WITH THE OTHERS.

PBBT! PBBT!
BUT THE BOYS WENT TOO FAR.

STOP IT!!! STOP!!!

AND MISS HEPLER GOT FIRED.

I'M WEARING GREEEEEN UNDERWEAR.

NOW I GET TO PINCH YOU SEVEN TIMES.
NO!

OH YEAH? PROVE IT!
OKAY!
GROSS, DON'T SHOW US!

LOOK! SHREEPY SHAWN ISN'T WEARING GREEN. GET HIM!
LEAVE ME ALONE!

A REAL COURTROOM! A CHANCE TO SEE THE JUSTICE SYSTEM IN ACTION!

WE'LL SCHEDULE THE PRETRIAL HEARING FOR APRIL 18. NEXT CASE.

WAIT... IS THAT...

MISS HEPLER?

MARIA HEPLER, YOU ARE CHARGED WITH TRESPASSING AND DESTRUCTION OF PROPERTY.

TRESPASSING? DESTRUCTION? THAT HAS NOTHING TO DO WITH GRABBING AARON.

OH MY GOSH, WHAT DID MISS HEPLER DO?

HOW DO YOU PLEAD?

NOT GUILTY.

VERY WELL. THE PRETRIAL HEARING IS SET FOR MAY 2.

NEXT CASE.

I NEVER FOUND OUT WHAT HAPPENED. I NEVER SAW HER AGAIN.

WHEN I WAS LITTLE, I THOUGHT MY TEACHERS LIVED AT SCHOOL.

I NEVER WONDERED ABOUT GROWN-UPS AND THEIR REAL LIVES.

OR THOUGHT MUCH ABOUT HOW I WOULD BE A GROWN-UP SOMEDAY.
WHAT'S THE MATTER?
HM?

I WANTED TO DO SO MUCH. I WANTED TO REACH FOR THE SKY.
OH, NOTHING.
BUT IT SEEMED LIKE THE RULES WOULDN'T LET GIRLS GO TOO FAR.

MY MOM'S GOING TO MARRY HIM, SO WE'RE MOVING TO CALIFORNIA.
OH NO!

I'M GOING TO HAVE STEP-SISTERS I'VE NEVER EVEN MET. IT'S SO WEIRD.

AMY, DON'T LEAVE ME!

SHUT UP, VANCE.

I'M GOING TO BE SO BORED WHEN YOU MOVE. WHAT IF MY NEW NEIGHBORS ARE TOTAL LOSERS?
YOU'LL GET OVER IT.

HEY SHANNON.
VANCE KNOWS MY NAME???

HEY VANCE.

VANCE WAS A SIXTH GRADER TOO, BUT WE'D NEVER BEEN IN THE SAME CLASS.

I WASN'T SURE IF HE WAS POPULAR.
HE JUST KINDA DID HIS OWN THING.

ARE YOU READY?

AAAAAHHHHHH!!!

WALK LIKE AN EGYPTIAN...

I LOVE THE BANGLES.
NO WAY! ME TOO! THAT'S SO COOL.

LOOK, YOU'RE MARRIED!

WHEN TWO PEOPLE WERE SWINGING EXACTLY IN SYNC...

...WE CALLED IT "BEING MARRIED."

ONLY LITTLE KIDS SAY THAT, AMY.

IT WAS JUST A JOKE.

LET'S GO INTO THE TREEHOUSE.

DO YOU LIKE VANCE?
GROSS, HE'S LIKE MY BROTHER.

TRUTH OR DARE.
TRUTH.

UM...DO YOU LIKE ANY GIRLS?

YES.
OH.

HEY, LOOK, PRINCESS LEIA FROM *JEDI*.
TRUTH OR DARE.

DARE.

I DARE YOU TO KISS ME.

YEAH, SO ANYWAY, I THINK *RETURN OF THE JEDI* IS THE BEST ONE.

HA! YOU'RE TOTALLY BLUSHING.
SHUT UP!

AMY?
JUST A SEC!

TRUTH.
I DIDN'T ASK—

WILL YOU GO WITH ME?

SHANNON?
I WAS SO SHOCKED.
I PRETENDED NOT TO HEAR.

YEAH?
I SAID, WILL YOU GO WITH ME?

OH! UM...UH...I'LL TELL YOU LATER.

COOL. HERE'S MY NUMBER.

And though she was far from her house, something deep inside Alexandra felt at home. Her essence was in harmony with Athridor. Perhaps here, at last, she wouldn't be a weirdo.

"It is you!" said a prince-in-exile. "The prophecy said a girl with hair like fire would help reunite the Emerald Star. Drithvan is looking for you."

"Don't worry," said the prince. "I will protect you."

Alexandra and the prince walked together and talked for hours. They felt like they had been friends forever.

"Lady Alexandra," said the prince, "I've been in exile for so long, I thought I would never be happy again."
"But I am enchanted by your powerful essence. Please, marry me."
"Marry you?" said Alexandra.

"But I'm just a normal girl back home. And I don't think I'm ready to get married, even to a prince."
The prince begged her to say yes to his offer of marriage.
Alexandra said she'd tell him later.

WENDY, I'M FREAKING OUT.

IS IT A BOY?
UM...
YEAH.
YES!!

HIS NAME IS VANCE, AND HE'S REALLY COOL. HE ASKED ME TO GO WITH HIM.
DID YOU SAY YES?
NOT YET.

AAAH!! YOU HAVE TO!!

BUT WHAT DOES IT EVEN MEAN TO GO WITH HIM? WHAT AM I SUPPOSED TO DO?
JUST CALL HIM. TALK TO HIM. TREAT HIM LIKE A PRINCE.

VANCE

VANCE?
THIS IS SHANNON. I JUST WAS CALLING TO TELL YOU...
...YES.
COOL.

SO...UM, WHAT'S YOUR FAVORITE MOVIE?
*THE BREAKFAST CLUB.*

I HAVEN'T SEEN THAT YET, BUT MY SISTER DID. SHE LIVES IN LOS ANGELES.

THAT'S COOL. SO WHAT'S YOUR FAVORITE MOVIE?
PROBABLY *GOONIES*. I SAW IT IN THE THEATER FOUR TIMES.

FINALLY I DIDN'T HAVE TO BE ASHAMED THAT NO BOYS LIKED ME.

HEY SHANNON!

IS IT TRUE?

BUT HAD I GOTTEN THIS ALL WRONG?
ARE YOU GOING WITH VANCE?
WHAT?
WAS THERE A NEW RULE? WAS GOING WITH A BOY BAD NOW? OR MAYBE JEN THOUGHT IT WAS EMBARRASSING TO GO WITH SOMEONE LIKE VANCE?

SIXTH GRADE FELT LIKE A MINEFIELD. ONE MISSTEP...

DANGER
MINEFIELD

UM...NO. I'M NOT. I'M TOTALLY NOT.

VANCE SAYS YOU CALLED HIM LAST NIGHT. HE SAYS YOU SAID YOU'D GO WITH HIM.
WELL, I'M NOT GOING WITH HIM, OKAY?

I FELT HORRIBLE FOR LYING, AND I DIDN'T EVEN KNOW WHY I'D DONE IT.

LYING HAD JUST FELT SAFER THAN TELLING THE TRUTH.

I THREW A GOING-AWAY PARTY FOR AMY IN MY BACKYARD.

AT MY NEW SCHOOL, SIXTH GRADE IS ALREADY PART OF JUNIOR HIGH.

YOU'LL COME BACK AND VISIT A LOT, RIGHT?
DEFINITELY!
I WAS REALLY GOING TO MISS AMY, BUT FOR THE FIRST TIME IN MY LIFE, I FELT LIKE I HAD FRIENDS TO SPARE.

HEY!
OH, HEY! YOU CAME!

JUSTIN WAS HAVING A PARTY AT HIS HOUSE SO I TOLD HIM THEY SHOULD JOIN US.

ARE WE CRASHING YOUR PARTY OR WHAT?
NO, IT'S OKAY.

SO...YOU GOT ANY MUSIC?

I'D NEVER HAD BOYS OVER BEFORE.

THANKS, MOM.

YOUR BOY FRIENDS JOINED YOU! HOW NICE.

...THEY'RE NOT OUR BOYFRIENDS, MOM...

OH, I JUST MEANT FRIENDS THAT ARE BOYS.

HEY, YOU KNOW WHAT? THIS YEAR WE SHOULD ALL GO TO LAGOON TOGETHER.
YEAH, IN ONE BIG GROUP!

I LOVE THIS SONG!
GIRLS JUST WANNA HAVE FUN!

COME ON.
UM...OKAY.

HEY GUYS, LOOK WHAT WE WORKED OUT.

NEW RULE: BOYS AND GIRLS CAN HANG OUT. AND IT CAN NOT BE AWKWARD AT ALL.

# Chapter Three

How are you feeling today?

☐ good

☐ bad

☐ way too complicated to even explain

MY MOM SAID YES TO GOING AROUND WITH YOU GUYS AT LAGOON ON SATURDAY.
ALL RIGHT!
I CAN'T BELIEVE YOUR PARENTS DIDN'T LET YOU GO TO AN AMUSEMENT PARK WITH FRIENDS.

LAGOON IS A "SPECIAL FAMILY DAY."
AND WE WERE TOO LITTLE.

BUT WE'RE NOT LITTLE ANYMORE.
THAT'S RIGHT!

I'VE ALWAYS HATED ROLLER COASTERS.

WHEN I WAS LITTLE, I LOVED LAGOON.
Welcome to Lagoon
WE ONLY GOT TO GO ONCE EACH YEAR, SO IT WAS AN EXCITING DAY.

MY HEART POUNDED. MY TUMMY DID FLIP-FLOPS.
I FELT GREAT.

GLUG GLUG GLUG

WHEEEE!
YAWN
PUTT
PUTT
PUTT

WENDY AND LAURA WANT US TO GO ON ONE OF THEIR RIDES, OKAY?

IT ISN'T A KIDDIE RIDE, BUT I THINK YOU'LL BE OKAY.

IT'S MORE FUN IF YOU SCREAM!

AAAAAAHHH!

THE AIR WAS ALL GONE. I COULDN'T BREATHE.

WHOOOOSH!!
I THOUGHT I WAS DYING.

SHANNON, WE'VE GOT TO GO.
IT WAS MY FIRST TIME ON A ROLLER COASTER.

WAAAH!!

AFTER THAT, ON OUR YEARLY TRIP TO LAGOON...
ISN'T THIS FUN?

WHEEEEE!
PUTT PUTT PUTT
...I ALWAYS TRIED TO STAY IN KIDDIE LAND.

UNTIL ONE YEAR...
YOU'RE TOO BIG FOR THIS.

YOU'RE TOO BIG FOR THIS.

SO MY MOM SAID I HAD TO START RIDING WITH MY OLDER SISTERS.

Colossus
I DIDN'T KNOW WHY I WAS SO SCARED.

MY SISTERS WEREN'T SCARED OF THE BIG RIDES WHEN THEY WERE MY AGE.

FIRE
WHEN THEY WENT ON RIDES TOO SCARY FOR ME, I TRIED JUST WAITING FOR THEM...

HEY GIRLIE.

WHAT ARE YOU DOING ALONE?

NEED COMPANY?
FIRE
BUT WAITING WAS SCARY TOO.

I KNEW IT WAS WEIRD HOW NERVOUS I GOT. NOT JUST AT LAGOON. ALL THE TIME.

BECAUSE OF ALL MY STOMACHACHES, MY MOM TOOK ME TO DOCTORS.
THEY DIDN'T SEEM TO KNOW WHAT WAS WRONG WITH ME.

IT'S PROBABLY JUST ANXIETY.
I DIDN'T REALLY UNDERSTAND WHAT "ANXIETY" WAS, BUT THEY MADE IT SOUND LIKE IT WASN'T A BIG DEAL.

THAT I SHOULD JUST IGNORE IT.

I TRIED.

THE SCARED, YUCKY, BAD FEELINGS THAT BUGGED ME AT LAGOON WERE A LOT LIKE HOW I FELT ALMOST EVERY DAY.

I DREADED THE FUN HOUSE BECAUSE I NEVER KNEW WHEN THOSE LOUD JETS OF AIR WOULD SHOOT OUT.
EVEN ON NORMAL DAYS, I OFTEN FELT THAT KIND OF DREAD, LIKE I WAS JUST WAITING FOR SOMETHING BAD TO HAPPEN.

EVEN THOUGH I KNEW IT WAS ALL FAKE, I WAS REALLY FRIGHTENED IN THE HAUNTED HOUSE RIDE.
IN NORMAL LIFE, I FELT AFRAID A LOT TOO, SOMETIMES FOR WHAT SEEMED LIKE NO REASON AT ALL.

AT LAGOON, THE TILT-A-WHIRL GAVE ME A SICK STOMACH.

AT HOME, ALL MY WORRYING MADE ME FEEL LIKE I WAS STILL ON THE TILT-A-WHIRL.

A LOT OF DAYS I FELT LIKE I DID ON THE ROLLER COASTER: TRAPPED. HELPLESS. MY WORRIES OUT OF MY CONTROL.

IT'S CONFUSING TO FEEL SICK AND AFRAID AND TRAPPED AND FULL OF DREAD WHEN YOU'RE NOT ON A RIDE...
...BUT JUST A KID GOING TO SCHOOL AND TRYING TO BE NORMAL.

ONE OF MY REGULAR WORRIES CAME FROM THE NEWS.

USA

USSR

USA

SPROING!!

WE HATE YOU. WE WANT TO DESTROY YOU. ALL OF YOU.

BUT I DIDN'T DO ANYTHING. I'M JUST A KID.

USA

WE DON'T CARE. WE HATE YOU! WE WILL DESTROY YOU!

HAVE A GOOD DAY!

IN FOURTH GRADE, THE BAD FEELINGS STARTED COMING WITH SCARY THOUGHTS.

this is the LAST TIME you'll EVER SEE your house it's going to BURN DOWN while you're at school and EVERY THING you know will be GONE GONE

WHEW.
PANT PANT

it's going to burn BURN BURN BURN

you better pray so hard or it'll be your fault

...PLEASE BLESS MY HOUSE THAT IT WON'T BURN DOWN...

SEE YOU AFTER SCHOOL!

this is the LAST TIME you will ever see your MOM and you are going to be SAD for the rest of your life

ALMOST EVERY DAY WHEN I WALKED HOME FROM SCHOOL, I WAS AFRAID I'D TURN THE LAST CORNER AND SEE A PILE OF ASH WHERE MY HOUSE HAD BEEN...

MOM? MOM?
...OR FIND MY MOM REALLY WAS GONE, JUST LIKE MY WORRIES WARNED SHE WOULD BE.

SHANNON?
SHE'S HERE! THE WORRIES WERE WRONG!

WHAT HAPPENED?
NOTHING.
MAYBE SHE'S OKAY BECAUSE I WORRIED. MAYBE I NEED TO KEEP WORRYING SO THAT SHE STAYS SAFE.

BY SIXTH GRADE, I WAS USED TO THE WORRIES. THEY WERE HARD TO EXPLAIN, SO I DIDN'T REALLY TALK ABOUT THEM. AND I KEPT TRYING TO IGNORE THEM.
IT DIDN'T WORK.

BUT SIXTH GRADE WAS THE YEAR I WAS SUPPOSED TO BE TOO BIG FOR ALL MY LITTLE-KID WORRIES.
THE BOYS SAID THEY'RE COMING WITH US.
KILLER!

SHANNON, YOU'RE COMING TO LAGOON TOO, RIGHT?
I CAN'T LET THEM KNOW I'M SCARED...
UM...YEAH. OF COURSE.

YEAH, IT'S GOING TO BE AWESOME!

"How did this shard of the Emerald Star come to me, I wonder?" asked Alexandra.

"I would guess the merpeople found you," said the noble girl.

"When Amerdath threw the Emerald Star into the ocean, the merpeople must have found it and kept it safe, till they could follow your essence and deliver to you one of the shards."

Alexandra wished she could meet the merpeople.

She would ask them if they ever felt cold in the deep, jewel-green waters...

...or how they went to the bathroom. Did they have toilets? Or did they just let it out anywhere?

And what did they eat? Fish? Just raw fish all the time?
you can't do this
"What was that?" asked Alexandra.

YOU CAN'T WRITE this story you're making lots of MISTAKES
NO ONE Would Want to read this you SHOULD QUIT

Quit QUIT QUIT Quit QUIT

DELETE
DELETE
DELETE

UGH, I CAN'T BELIEVE IT'S ONLY WEDNESDAY. THIS WEEK IS MOVING SOOO SLOW.

YOU KNOW WHAT WOULD BE FUNNY?

WE SHOULD TALK ABOUT OURSELVES IN THE THIRD PERSON FOR THE REST OF THE WEEK.

SHANNON IS SO BORED. SHANNON WISHES SOMEONE WOULD ENTERTAIN HER.

UM...

OR WE COULD MAKE UP A FAKE PERSON AND KEEP TALKING ABOUT HER ALL THE TIME AND MAKE PEOPLE WONDER! WE COULD CALL HER...

...MRS. BUTTOCKS!

REMEMBER THAT TIME MRS. BUTTOCKS THREW THAT BIG PARTY AND RENTED ALL THOSE MONKEYS TO BE WAITERS?

I SWEAR, MRS. BUTTOCKS ALWAYS SMELLS LIKE PICKLES AND SOCKS—
UM, SHANNON?
I DON'T REALLY WANT TO DO THIS.

OH! OKAY.

WHEN I DIDN'T FEEL GOOD, WHEN I WAS HAVING TROUBLE WITH FRIENDS, MY WORRIES GOT STRONGER.

7x1/6
10x3/7

IS YOUR MOM DEAD?
7x1/6

IS YOUR MOM DEAD?
SOMETIMES AWFUL THOUGHTS GOT STUCK IN MY HEAD.

3x5/6
9x1/2
I'D TRY NOT TO THINK ABOUT THEM.

YOUR DEAD?
5 x 2/3
BUT THEY JUST KEPT COMING, AROUND AND AROUND...

IS YOUR MOM DEAD?
...AND AROUND...

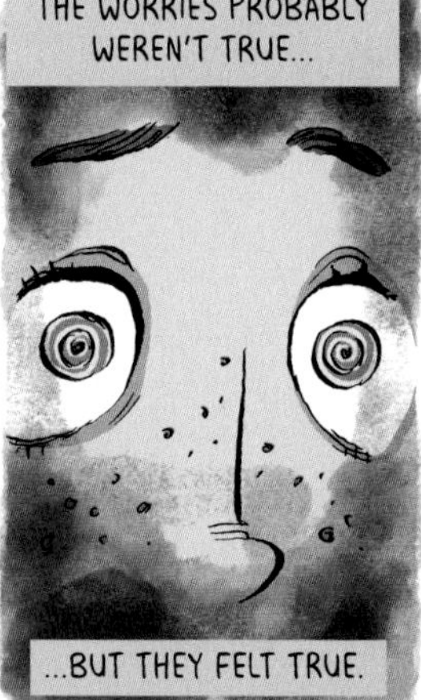
I KNEW BY NOW THAT THE WORRIES PROBABLY WEREN'T TRUE...
...BUT THEY FELT TRUE.

SHANNON?

HOW ABOUT YOU JOIN THE REST OF US AND DO YOUR MATH INSTEAD OF DAYDREAMING?

stupid
stupid

BRRINGG!!!

YOU'RE NOT UPSET ABOUT MRS. GRANGER, ARE YOU?
everyone thinks you're STUPID

STUPID
STUPID
NOPE.

everybody is FINE
what's WRONG with
you...?
TRYING TO IGNORE THE THOUGHTS AND FEELINGS FELT LIKE SITTING IN A HOUSE ON FIRE AND PRETENDING IT WASN'T BURNING.

of course
your house didn't
BURN DOWN
STUPID STUPID
stupid

stupid stupid stupid

SHANNON?

STUPID

CRASH!

WHAT HAPPENED?

NOTHING! NOTHING, OKAY?

AFTER ALL DAY AT SCHOOL, TRYING TO HOLD IN THOSE FEELINGS...
I DON'T LIKE THAT TONE!
JUST LEAVE ME ALONE!

...BY THE TIME I GOT HOME, I WAS EXHAUSTED.

SLAM

MOM PROBABLY HATES ME NOW TOO.
I FELT LIKE I HAD TO KEEP REMEMBERING ALL MY MISTAKES.
But you still feel BAD and you can't FEEL BAD for no reason there must be REASON you FEEL BAD so let's THINK about EVERYTHING WRONG you've EVER DONE
SO THAT I COULD BE FORGIVEN. SO THAT I WOULDN'T MAKE MISTAKES EVER AGAIN.
remember that time in first grade you were mean to Peter and you NEVER said SORRY and don't forget how you LIED to Mrs. Johnson when she asked if you left a paper towel by the sink and what about second grade when you FORGOT to take a present to Natalie's birthday and you said you'd bring it LATER but you NEVER did you were BAD BAD BAD BAD

WE SHOULD GO NOW BEFORE THE LINES GET LONG.
OKAY.

CLANG!!
CLANG!!
ALL MY FEELINGS WERE WARNING ME THAT TODAY WAS GOING TO BE REALLY BAD.

CLANG CLANG CLANG CLANG
BUT THEY DID THAT A LOT.

SO I TRIED TO IGNORE IT.

ALSO, I HAD TO TOUCH ALL MY STUFFED ANIMALS BEFORE LEAVING MY ROOM.

IF I DIDN'T FEEL COMPLETE...

...I HAD TO TOUCH THEM ALL AGAIN.

I DIDN'T KNOW WHY.

SHANNON, ARE YOU COMING?

JUST A SEC!

SHEESH, WHAT TOOK YOU SO LONG?

I JUST HAD...TO DO SOME STUFF.

SHANNON, YOU HAVE TWO SPEEDS: SLOW AND STOP.

Welcome to
Lagoon

THERE THEY ARE!

MEET US AT THE PICNIC AREA FOR DINNER.
OKAY!

NO ONE'S TALKING ABOUT GOING ON ROLLER COASTERS. MAYBE TODAY WON'T BE HORRIBLE AFTER ALL!

HEY, WE SHOULD PLAY!

DING!

LET'S PLAY AGAIN.

DING!

HEY HEY, GO GO...

YES!
YAY!
GOOD JOB!
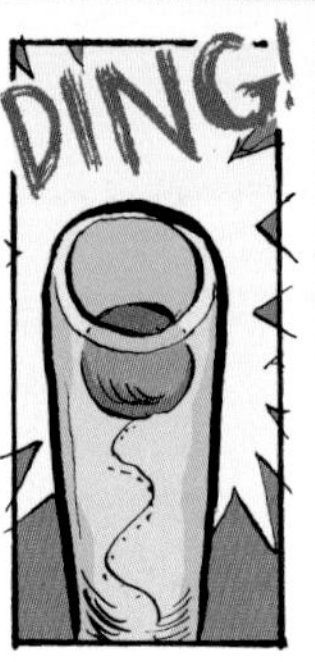
DING!

HERE.

THANKS.

I WON THIS FOR YOU.
THANKS.
FOR YOU, MY LADY.
WOW!
YOU CAN HAVE THIS.
OKAY.

THEY'RE ALL IDENTICAL.
YEAH, OUR BEARS ARE QUADRUPLETS.

HEY GUYS!
EMILY! YOU MADE IT.

HANG ON ONE SEC.

HERE.
COOL.

THEY'RE QUINTUPLETS NOW!
TOTALLY.

HI! SHANNON!

OH! HEY. HI MOM...

SOB...

ICEE
ICEE
ICEE
OP IT

ROLLER
COASTER

HEY, WHERE'D YOU GO?

JUST...TALKING TO MY MOM.

I COULDN'T TELL WHEN NICOLE REALLY WANTED TO KNOW HOW I WAS FEELING...
YOU OKAY?

SURE.
...OR WHEN SHE WAS ASKING SO SHE COULD TELL JEN ABOUT ME LATER.

YOU SEEM UPSET.

NO, I'M FINE. REALLY.
6
5
4
3

AAAAAAHHHHH

AAA

AAAAHH!

AAAAH!!!

EEEEEE!!!

AAAAAAHHHHH

I LOVE LAGOON.
YEAH.

AREN'T THE BOYS BEING SOOOO NICE?
YEP.

HEY LOOK, IT'S VANCE.

WHERE?

THIRSTY?

ARE YOU CRYING?
NO!

IT'S JUST THE STUPID SQUIRT GUN WATER.

SO FUN!
YEP. SO FUN.
FUN HOUSE NEXT!

THAT'S HER?
YEAH, THAT'S HER.

HEY GIRL.

"I'm not ready to get married, Your Highness," said Alexandra. "Can we be friends?"
The prince's charming smile turned as sour as lemonade without the sugar.

"You dare to insult me?" he said. "I never want to see your ugly face again!"

"Your insults sting," said Alexandra, "but they cannot harm my essence. And my realm is greater than yours, for my kingdom is magic!"

Just then, Alexandra heard screams.
Drithvan's soldiers were attacking the camp.

"We'll save you!" said all the boys.

And they stood in front of the girls and fought.

"Help!" Alexandra said, but no one came to fight for her.
"Tell me," Alexandra whispered to her reflection in the mirror, curiously, almost demanding.
"Tell me about my powers and what I can do with them. Tell me!"

A voice came into her mind.
A strong voice with no fear
and no bad feelings.
"Look into your
heart, fire child.
Find yourself."

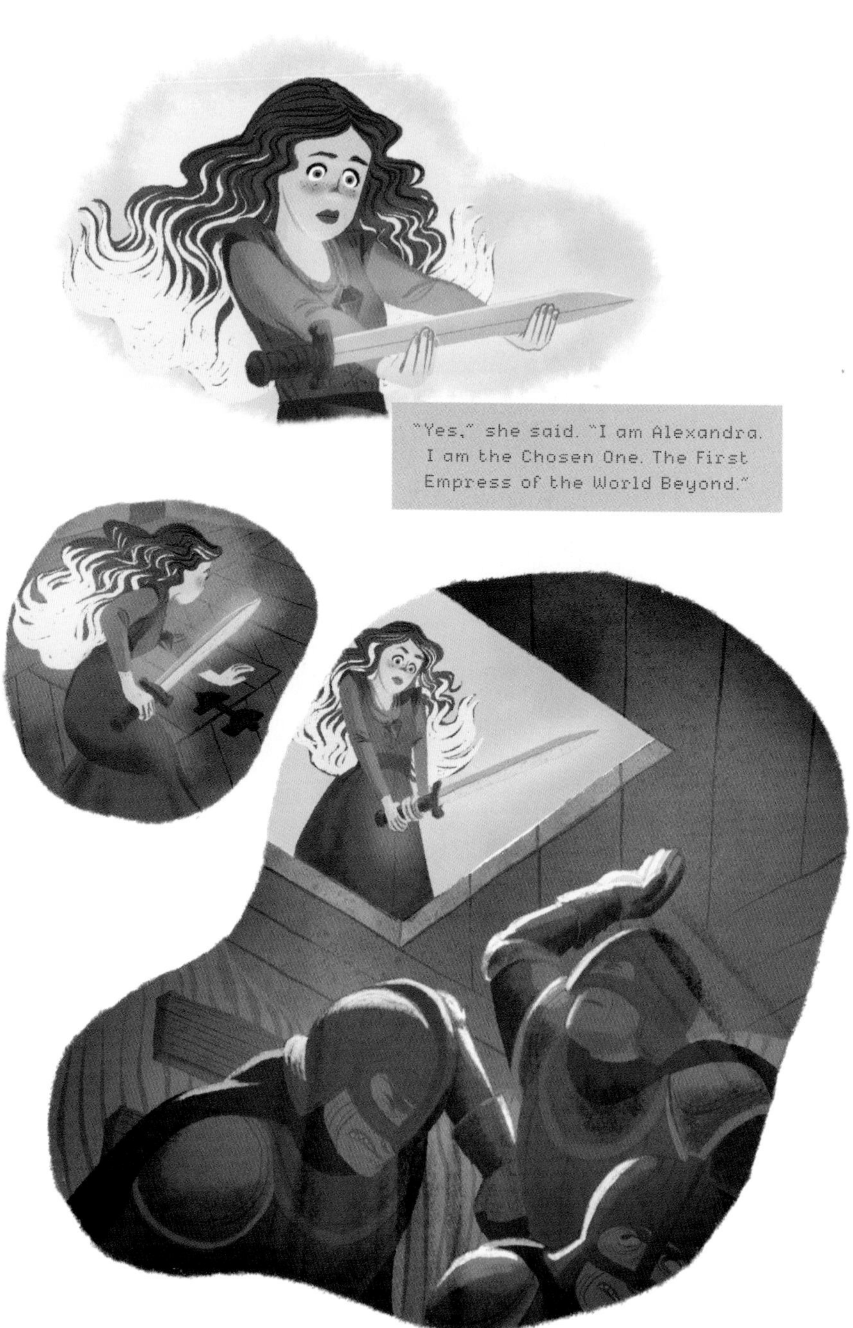
"Yes," she said. "I am Alexandra.
I am the Chosen One. The First
Empress of the World Beyond."

"And I am not
afraid!"

# Chapter Four

Are we still best friends?

- ☐ yes
- ☐ no
- ☐ I'm not sure

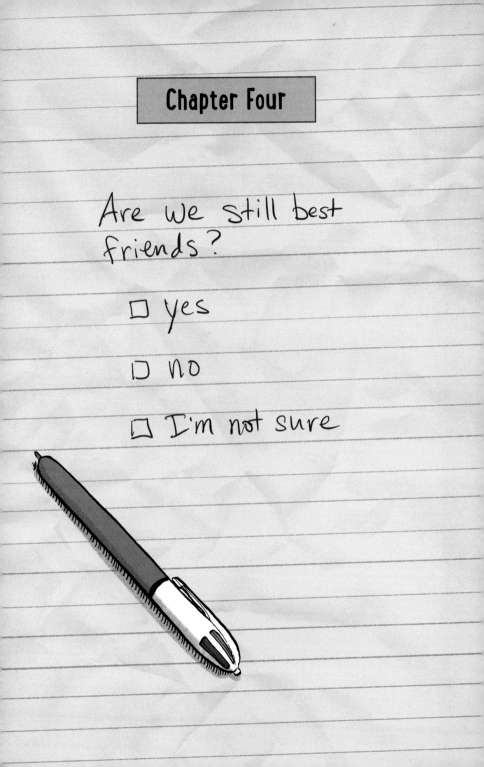

SIXTH GRADE WAS ALMOST OVER.
HEY, WAIT UP!
AFTER SUMMER, WE'D START JUNIOR HIGH.

SORRY, I HAD TO STOP IN THE BATHROOM.
AUNT FLO CAME TO VISIT.

AUNT FLO?
HER PERIOD.
NICOLE'S ON HER PERIOD AGAIN.

WAIT, NICOLE ALREADY STARTED HER PERIOD?
WAIT, AM I THE ONLY ONE WHO HASN'T?

DID YOU HEAR ABOUT JOHN BRADFORD'S OLDER BROTHER?
NO...

SOME EIGHTH GRADERS BEAT HIM UP WHEN HE WAS WALKING HOME AFTER SCHOOL.
WHY? IS HE OKAY?

THEY BROKE HIS RIBS.
AND HIS JAW. THE DOCTORS HAD TO WIRE IT SHUT. HE CAN ONLY EAT FOOD THAT'S BEEN THROUGH A BLENDER.
THAT...SOUNDS REALLY SCARY.

I DON'T THINK THE EIGHTH GRADERS WILL BEAT ME UP. I MEAN, EVERYBODY KNOWS MY BIG BROTHER AND SISTER.
MAYBE BEING BEST FRIENDS WITH JEN WOULD KEEP ME SAFE TOO.

ALL YEAR WE'D BEEN THE OLDEST IN THE SCHOOL. BUT SOON WE'D BE THE YOUNGEST AGAIN.

DO YOU GUYS WANT TO PLAY MONSTER SOCCER OR SOMETHING?

LET'S DO A HUMAN CHAIN AGAIN!

YEAH!
OKAY!

HOW ABOUT THIS TIME WE GET EVERYBODY.
EVERYBODY?

YEAH, LIKE THE ENTIRE SIXTH GRADE! AND FIFTH GRADERS AND FOURTH GRADERS TOO!
EVERYBODY!

WELL, NOT EVERYBODY. JUST PEOPLE WE LIKE.
YEAH, OR WHAT'S THE POINT?

I GUESS THE POINT WAS THAT WE WERE POPULAR.

AND THEY WEREN'T.

I COULDN'T BE POPULAR UNLESS SOME PEOPLE WERE UNPOPULAR.

I JUST MEAN, IT'D BE FUN TO SEE HOW MANY PEOPLE WE COULD GET IN THE CHAIN. LIKE A WORLD RECORD!
WELL, THERE'S SOME PEOPLE WHO I DON'T WANT TO TOUCH.

LIKE CRYSTAL.
TOTALLY.

SHE DRESSES LIKE A WEIRDO. AND I BET SHE NEVER SHOWERS.
MY SISTER SAYS HER BROTHER IS A TOTAL LOSER TOO.

LIKE, HOW IS HE A LOSER?
HE DRESSES LIKE A ROCKER, BUT A FAKE ROCKER.

OH, THAT'S BAD.

SNIFF
-SOB-

CRYSTAL!

WE WEREN'T TALKING ABOUT YOU. WE WERE TALKING ABOUT...
...A DIFFERENT CRYSTAL FROM OUR NEIGHBORHOOD—

OH NO.
WE SHOULD APOLOGIZE.

HEY CRYSTAL?
WE'RE REALLY SORRY WE MADE YOU—

JUST SHUT UP.

CRYSTAL, I SWEAR, WE DIDN'T—

SHUT UP, SHANNON, AND NEVER TALK TO ME AGAIN!
SLAM!

WOW.
I DIDN'T USED TO THINK I WAS MEAN.

SHE IS EVEN WORSE THAN I THOUGHT.
BUT MAYBE I WAS WRONG.

WE'RE OUT OF LOCKER CANDY.
WELL, THE YEAR IS ALMOST OVER.

JEN, CAN I ASK YOU SOMETHING?

ARE WE STILL BEST FRIENDS?

I MEAN, SURE, WE'RE FRIENDS.
BUT WE'RE TOO OLD NOW TO HAVE BEST FRIENDS, RIGHT?

WE'RE GOING CAMPING NEXT WEEKEND.
YEAH.
COOL.

WOULD YOU EACH LIKE TO INVITE A FRIEND?

REALLY?

WE'D NEVER BEEN ABLE TO BRING A FRIEND ON A FAMILY TRIP BEFORE.

WHO SHOULD I INVITE?

VERY COOL
EVERYONE WILL THINK I'M COOL IF SHE COMES.
WE HAVE FUN TOGETHER SOMETIMES.
DOESN'T LIKE MY GAMES
NOT MY BEST FRIEND ANYMORE?

MAYBE IF I INVITE HER WE'LL BECOME BETTER FRIENDS?
MAYBE SHE'LL BE NICER TO ME?
BUT WHAT IF SHE'S MEAN?

SOMETIMES REALLY NICE
I LOVE IT WHEN I GET HER LAUGHING SO HARD.
SHE KINDA LIKES IT WHEN THERE'S FRIENDSHIP DRAMA.

I'D BEEN FEELING GREAT ABOUT HAVING SO MANY FRIENDS.
BUT MAYBE THE FRIENDS I HAD WEREN'T REALLY CLOSE FRIENDS. GOOD FRIENDS.

PHOTOS

I MISSED HAVING A BEST FRIEND.
Kindergar
SOMEONE WHO GOT ME.
lloween!
WHO ALWAYS SEEMED TO LIKE ME.

ADRIENNE AND I HAD BEEN BEST FRIENDS SINCE KINDERGARTEN.

Make new friends
But keep the old
One is silver
And the other is gold
MAYBE WE'D STILL BE BEST FRIENDS IF SHE HADN'T MOVED TO A NEW SCHOOL.

I INVITED ADRIENNE, AND I KNEW IT WAS GOING TO BE JUST LIKE OLD TIMES.

I'M GETTING SLEEPY.

snore!

HOW'S YOUR SCHOOL?
GREAT. I LOVE IT.

WHOA.
DO YOU THINK THESE BOULDERS FELL OUT OF THE MOUNTAIN BACK WHEN JESUS DIED? LIKE, WHEN THE EARTH GROANED AT HIS DEATH?

UMM...NO.

WHAT DO YOU THINK WOULD BE THE WORST WAY TO DIE? MAYBE EATEN ALIVE BY ANTS? LIKE, MILLIONS OF TINY ANTS?

EW.

HEY, WHAT ARE YOU GUYS DOING?

JUST PLAYING.
WANNA WALK DOWN TO THE LAKE?

NOT REALLY.
OH.

YOU ARE SO PRETTY, ADRIENNE.
THANKS.

NO, SERIOUSLY, YOU LOOK LIKE A MODEL!

SERIOUSLY, SO SO PRETTY.

IT WENT ON LIKE THAT FOR A COUPLE OF DAYS.

YOU'RE, LIKE, TRYING WAY TOO HARD.
BUT I DON'T KNOW WHAT TO DO.

YOU SHOULD TALK TO HER.

I FEEL LIKE YOU'D RATHER PLAY WITH MY LITTLE SISTER THAN WITH ME.

WELL, I DIDN'T LOVE IT WHEN YOU FELL ASLEEP IN THE CAR, AND I HAD NOTHING TO DO.
SORRY. THE CARSICKNESS PILL MADE ME SLEEPY.

IT JUST SEEMS LIKE WE HAVE NOTHING TO TALK ABOUT.

I'M GOING TO GET SOME WATER.

Alexandra left the spy camp
and searched the jungle.
"Shasta!" Alexandra called out.
But there was no roar in reply.

Alexandra had never felt so alone, not even at boarding school when all the other girls had gone home for Christmas.
"There are others like me out there," said Alexandra. "Somewhere. I can feel it."
Alexandra fell into a trance. With deep thoughts, she called a name she knew not.

Then she felt it, like a bolt of lightning. Two minds locked together in power.
"Hello, I hear you," a girl's voice spoke into her mind.

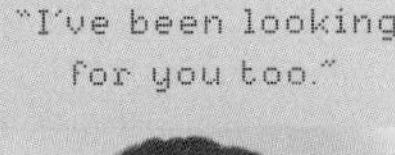
"I've been looking for you too."

"I'm Alexandra!" she said with her thoughts. "You must be the Second Empress."
"I can feel that our essence is in sync," said the girl.

"I feel the same way!" Alexandra answered with her thoughts. "We'd probably have a lot to talk about."

Two more voices entered her mind, two more girls who possessed a kindred essence.
"Regular people will never really understand us," came the voice of another girl into Alexandra's mind. "We need to find each other."

"A prophecy says, 'The daughters of Amerdath shall join as one, as the horizon joins the land and sun.'"

In that moment, Alexandra understood that she had at last found true friends.

Drithvan wanted to keep them apart, because together, they would be even mightier than he could imagine.

All of a sudden, a deep horror overtook Alexandra. It felt as if a vine wrapped around her and squeezed all her strength.

"I am Drithvan," echoed a voice inside her mind.

"And I have finally found you."

"No, you haven't!" Alexandra screamed back.
"You'll never get us, you'll never find us!"

She released a burst of the mighty power within her. The laughter stopped! The dark thoughts were gone.

But so too were the voices of the other girls.

"I will find you, my true friends," said Alexandra.

"And together we will free this world from Drithvan's evil power."

SHANNON!
I HAVE A NEW BOOK FOR YOU!

REALLY?
WILL THE JUNIOR HIGH LIBRARIAN GIVE ME BOOKS SHE THINKS I'LL LIKE TOO?

WILL THE JUNIOR HIGH EVEN HAVE A LIBRARY???

I REMEMBERED HOW MUCH YOU LIKED THE OTHER ROBIN MCKINLEY BOOK.

SO I SET THE NEW ONE ASIDE FOR YOU AS SOON AS WE GOT IT IN.
THE HERO AND THE CROWN
ROBIN McKINLEY

WAIT, IS ROBIN MCKINLEY IS STILL ALIVE?
UH-HUH, AND WRITING NEW BOOKS.

I GUESS I THOUGHT AUTHORS ONLY EXISTED LONG AGO AND FAR AWAY.

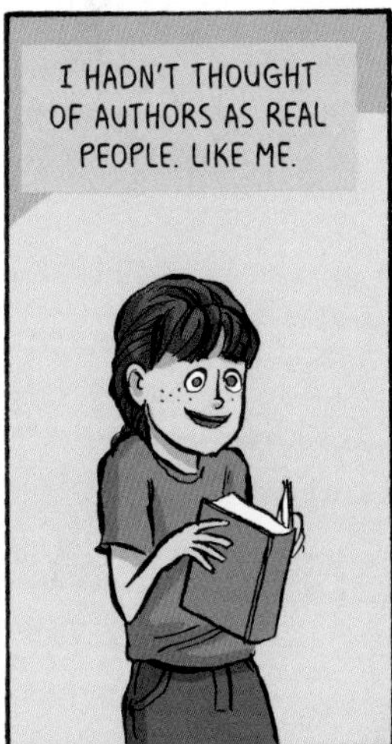
I HADN'T THOUGHT OF AUTHORS AS REAL PEOPLE. LIKE ME.

WOW! THE MAIN CHARACTER IS A REDHEAD!

SORRY.
OOPS.

YOU READ A LOT, DON'T YOU?

I GUESS...
YEAH, I USED TO LIKE READING TOO.

BUT MY BIG SISTER SAYS BY HIGH SCHOOL EVERYONE GROWS OUT OF IT.

ALL THE RULES FOR GIRLS SEEMED TO SAY I SHOULD CARE WHAT BOYS THOUGHT ABOUT ME.

AND I SHOULD TRY TO BE THE KIND OF GIRL THAT BOYS WOULD LIKE.

BUT...
EVERYONE GROWS OUT OF LIKING TO READ?

THAT DOESN'T SOUND RIGHT.

BESIDES, THE GIRL IN THE BOOK DIDN'T CARE WHAT BOYS THOUGHT ABOUT HER. SHE MOSTLY JUST WANTED TO RIDE HORSES AND FIGHT DRAGONS.

BRIIINGG!!

SHANNON?

MRS. GRANGER HAD HER BABY, SO MRS. ROSE WAS GOING TO BE OUR TEACHER FOR THE REST OF THE YEAR.

YOUR PAPER ON MEXICO WAS REALLY GOOD. YOU WRITE SUCH LOVELY IMAGERY.
THANKS! UM...

...I'M WRITING A BOOK TOO.

WHAT KIND?
A FANTASY.
WOW!

WELL, I'D LOVE TO READ WHAT YOU HAVE.
REALLY? REALLY-REALLY?

REALLY-REALLY.

ZZZZZ BEEP
ZZZZZ BEEP

If this is all your own work, Shannon, it's outstanding.

If this is all your own work, Shannon, it's outstanding.

MRS. ROSE?

IT IS ALL MY OWN WORK. I SWEAR. I DIDN'T COPY ANY OF IT.

WELL, YOU SHOULD BE VERY PROUD. KEEP WRITING.

I WILL! I...
I WANT TO BE A WRITER WHEN I GROW UP.

THE EVIDENCE WOULD SUGGEST THAT YOU ALREADY ARE A WRITER.
OH!

I AM A WRITER.

I'M SO GLAD YOU CAME TO OUR CLASS. I DON'T THINK MRS. GRANGER LIKED ME VERY MUCH.
I EXPECTED HER TO SAY "I'M SURE SHE DID" JUST TO BE NICE, OR MAYBE "WELL, WHAT DID YOU DO TO MAKE HER NOT LIKE YOU?" LIKE SOME ADULTS MIGHT...

BUT INSTEAD—
MAYBE NOT.

BUT IF SHE DIDN'T, THAT'S NOT YOUR FAULT.

SOME TEACHERS AND SOME STUDENTS JUST AREN'T A GOOD FIT FOR EACH OTHER.
OH. OKAY.

I'D NEVER HEARD A GROWN-UP SAY ANYTHING LIKE THAT BEFORE. IT FELT LIKE SUCH A RELIEF!

SOMETIMES IT'S LIKE THAT WITH FRIENDS.
WHAT IS?

IT'S NOBODY'S FAULT, BUT SOME FRIENDS JUST AREN'T A GOOD FIT FOR EACH OTHER EITHER.

YES, I THINK THAT'S TRUE.

I MISS MRS. GRANGER SOOO MUCH.
ME TOO. I LIKE HER WAY BETTER THAN MRS. ROSE.

REALLY?

DON'T YOU LIKE MRS. GRANGER BETTER TOO?

DANGER MINEFIELD

I DON'T KNOW.

OH MY GOSH, DO YOU LOVE THAT NEW WHITNEY HOUSTON SONG?
IT'S SO GOOD.

WHAT DO YOU THINK ABOUT IT, SHANNON?

HONESTLY?
I DON'T KNOW WHAT YOU'RE TALKING ABOUT, AND TRYING TO KEEP UP WITH EVERYTHING IS EXHAUSTING.

UM...OKAY.

FOR AN END-OF-YEAR CELEBRATION, WE TOOK A FIELD TRIP ON A STEAM TRAIN.
HEBER CITY

HEY SHAWN, CAN I SIT HERE?

SURE...

LADIES AND GENTLEMEN!

PRESENTING THE HOTTEST NEW ROCK-AND-ROLL BAND, SPARKLY BUTT!

AND OUR NEWEST MEMBER...

SHAWESOME SHAWN!

HEY BOY-O...

COME ON AND SING-A-LO-ONG!!

WOO!!
YEAH!!!

WOOO!!!

THAT WAS SO GREAT, AARON.

YEAH, SPARKLY BUTT IS GONNA BE HUGE.

YEAH, SPARKLY BUTT. AND EVERYTHING YOU DID.

I SHOULD'VE SPOKEN UP ABOUT SHAWN A LONG TIME AGO. I SHOULD'VE BEEN BRAVER.

MAYBE EVERYBODY FELT BAD FOR SHAWN TOO. MAYBE WE WERE ALL JUST TOO SCARED TO SAY ANYTHING.

THERE'S NO MORE ROOM.

BUT I RODE UP IN JEN'S VAN.

WELL, SORRY, ALL THE SEATS ARE TAKEN NOW.

JANE'S MOM HAS ROOM IN HER CAR.

CAN I RIDE BACK WITH YOU?

SURE, CLIMB IN!

BIG TIME...

BIG TIME!

SLEDGE HAMMER!

SORRY YOU HAD TO RIDE WITH JANE. SHE'S KIND OF WEIRD.
YEAH...

NO, ACTUALLY, SHE'S NOT WEIRD...

I MEAN, SHE IS BUT SO IS EVERYONE ELSE. I MEAN, WE'RE ALL WEIRD SORT OF, AREN'T WE?

OKAY...
WERE THESE FRIENDS RIGHT FOR ME?

THEY WERE POPULAR! AND THEY LIKED ME...SOMETIMES.

I DIDN'T FEEL RIGHT WITH THE GROUP, BUT I WASN'T SURE I COULD TRUST MY ROLLER-COASTER FEELINGS.

MAYBE FRIENDSHIP WAS SUPPOSED TO BE LIKE THIS.

ACHERS
OUNGE
DURING THE SUMMER, I WORKED IN THE SCHOOL LIBRARY AGAIN.

THIS YEAR, JENNY WAS THERE TOO.

DO YOU REMEMBER IN THIRD GRADE WHEN THAT POETRY GUY VISITED OUR CLASS?

OH YEAH, THAT WAS GREAT.

YOU SAID SOMETHING ABOUT A POEM, AND HE SAID, "YOU'RE VERY OBSERVANT."
HUH.
I DON'T REMEMBER.

I DO. I RAISED MY HAND AND ANSWERED THE NEXT QUESTION. I WANTED HIM TO TELL ME THAT I WAS OBSERVANT.

BUT HE DIDN'T.

IS...IS THAT PART OF THE REASON WHY YOU'VE NEVER LIKED ME?

I DON'T KNOW.

I GUESS I COULD UNDERSTAND THAT. THERE WERE A LOT OF THINGS I DIDN'T KNOW.

I DIDN'T KNOW WHY JENNY WAS THE WAY SHE WAS.

I DIDN'T KNOW WHY JEN WAS THE WAY SHE WAS EITHER.

6th Grade RULES!

OR IF JEN NOTICED HOW EVERYONE WENT ALONG WITH WHATEVER SHE SAID.

summertime
I DIDN'T KNOW HOW ADRIENNE AND I COULD HAVE BEEN BEST FRIENDS FOR SO MANY YEARS...

...AND THEN JUST NOT CLICK ANYMORE.

I DIDN'T KNOW WHY I SOMETIMES COULDN'T GET WORRIES OR SCARY THOUGHTS OUT OF MY HEAD. WAS EVERYONE LIKE THAT?
Welcome to Lagoon

FAMILY
I DIDN'T KNOW IF EVERYONE FELT LIKE THE WEIRDO IN THEIR FAMILY. OR IF I WAS THE ONLY ONE.

I DIDN'T KNOW IF I WAS PRETTY OR NOT. IF BOYS LIKED ME OR NOT.
with the boys!
OR IF ANY OF THAT EVEN MATTERED.

LOOK out, Bryant,
I DIDN'T KNOW IF JUNIOR HIGH WOULD BE GOOD. OR BETTER. OR AWFUL. OR SCARY.

RING
NOTES
AND I DEFINITELY DIDN'T KNOW IF I WOULD REALLY, TRULY GROW UP TO BE A WRITER.

HELLO?

I GOT IT IN THE MAIL! COME OVER TO NICOLE'S!
OKAY!

SO THESE ARE THE REQUIRED CLASSES. WE HAVE TO TAKE ONE OF EACH—ENGLISH, HEALTH, MATH, SOCIAL STUDIES, AND P.E.

AND THESE ARE THE ELECTIVES.
WE GET TWO ELECTIVES? LIKE, ANY CLASS WE WANT, WE JUST GET TO CHOOSE AND—

OH MY GOSH, THERE'S A DRAMA CLASS.

PLAYS!

ACTING!

THEATER!

LET'S TAKE GLEE FOR OUR FIRST ELECTIVE.
YEAH!
AND HOME EC FOR OUR SECOND.

NOT DRAMA?

NAH.

AND IF WE ALL PUT IN FOR ENGLISH 7 AND ALGEBRA 1, THAT MEANS WE'LL HAVE AT LEAST THREE CLASSES TOGETHER, PLUS WE'LL BE ON THE SAME LUNCH.
YEAH!

BUT IT SAYS THAT HONORS ENGLISH HAS A UNIT ON CREATIVE WRITING, AND THAT CLASS GETS TO HELP MAKE A LITERARY MAGAZINE.

SOUNDS LIKE IT'D HAVE A LOT OF HOMEWORK.
DON'T YOU WANT TO DO DRAMA?

ACTING AND STUFF, LIKE THE GAMES WE USED TO PLAY!

AND WITH CREATIVE WRITING WE COULD KEEP WRITING STORIES! REMEMBER THAT BOOK WE WROTE TOGETHER IN FOURTH GRADE?

UM, THAT WAS MOSTLY YOU.
YEAH, IN FIFTH, SHANNON TRIED TO GET ME TO WRITE A BOOK WITH HER TOO!

OOH! IF WE'RE ALL IN GLEE, HOME EC, ENGLISH 7, AND ALGEBRA 1, THE ONLY HEALTH LEFT IS THIRD PERIOD—

SO THAT'S FIVE CLASSES TOGETHER!
PLUS THERE'S A GOOD CHANCE WE'D ALL BE IN THE SAME P.E. AND SOCIAL STUDIES.
THIS IS GOING TO BE AMAZING.

IF I SIGNED UP FOR HONORS ENGLISH AND DRAMA...
...I PROBABLY WOULDN'T HAVE ANY CLASSES WITH THEM.

THE THOUGHT OF STARTING JUNIOR HIGH WITHOUT ANY FRIENDS IN MY CLASSES FELT LIKE...

GLEE IS GOING TO BE SO FUN. REMEMBER THAT SONG WE LEARNED AT CAMP?

"MAKE NEW FRIENDS BUT KEEP THE OLD..."
"...ONE IS SILVER AND THE OTHER IS GOLD."
LET'S DO A ROUND!

"MAKE NEW FRIENDS BUT—"

"—KEEP THE OLD..."
"MAKE NEW FRIENDS BUT—"

"ONE IS SILVER AND—"
"MAKE NEW FRIENDS BUT—"
"—KEEP THE OLD..."

MAKE NEW FRIENDS, BUT...

MAKE NEW FRIENDS?

...THEY INVITED THE WHOLE MODELING AGENCY TO THE PARTY, I GUESS SO THERE WOULD BE LOTS OF PRETTY GIRLS.
WEIRD.

YEAH, THAT'S L.A. WEIRD. I DANCED WITH A MOVIE STAR. BUT YOU PROBABLY WOULDN'T KNOW WHO HE IS.
BUT THAT'S SO COOL!

I GUESS. HE WAS A JERK.

ARE YOU GLAD YOU MOVED TO L.A.?
I MEAN, SURE, YEAH.

IT'S JUST...IT WOULD FEEL SCARY TO ME. TO BE ON MY OWN LIKE THAT.
IT IS. I'M CRAZY BROKE AND THE MODELING STUFF STINKS, BUT I HAD TO MAKE A BIG CHANGE, YOU KNOW?

YEAH...

THE LAST DAY OF SUMMER. THE GROUP WAS GETTING TOGETHER, BUT I DECIDED TO KEEP MY OWN TRADITION.

SPRITE AND UNSALTED SALTINES WERE WHAT I ALWAYS ATE WHEN I WAS SICK. I WASN'T SICK, BUT I STILL WANTED SOME COMFORT.

GOOD LUCK! SEE YOU AFTER SCHOOL!

STUPID WORRIES.

317
313

And so she set off on a new adventure.

She had trained for this day. Though she had many scars, they no longer ached.

She knew this quest would take her down long, lonely roads.

She knew there would be danger.

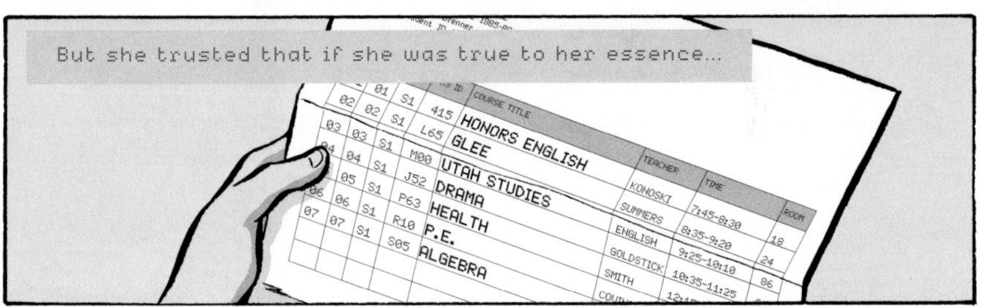
But she trusted that if she was true to her essence...
COURSE TITLE
TEACHER
TIME
ROOM
HONORS ENGLISH
GLEE
UTAH STUDIES
DRAMA
HEALTH
P.E.
ALGEBRA
KONOSKI
SUMMERS
ENGLISH
GOLDSTICK
SMITH
7:45-8:30
8:35-9:20
9:25-10:10
10:35-11:25
18
24
86

...she would meet like minds and kindred spirits.
Honors English
and
Creative Writing

She would find friends to keep her company even in the darkest hours.

And she would fight a path to victory.

# Hey you,

Sixth grade would have been a lot easier if I'd always known exactly the right things to say and do. Even though I wasn't perfect, I still wanted to tell you the truth of what I did and how I felt. When I was eleven and twelve, I was trying to figure out a lot of things: Is there only one right way to be a girl? How grown-up should I try to be? How can you tell which friends are good friends? Why do I feel so weird and sad sometimes? Why don't some people get along? When is it time to let go of friends who don't quite get you?

I tried to answer these questions for myself. Sometimes there was no right or wrong answer, so I just had to do my best. And sometimes, I just plain messed up. I think that's okay. Part of growing up is making mistakes. I'm lucky that I had people in my life who loved me no matter what.

When I was a kid, I didn't have a name for those yucky feelings, ideas, and worries that bothered me almost every day. I now know that it's called anxiety. And some of the things I did—like needing to touch all my stuffed animals in order to feel "complete"—are behaviors typical of obsessive-compulsive disorder. But not everybody who has anxiety or OCD experiences it in exactly the same way I did.

Anxiety is a totally normal feeling, and like all feelings, it's important. It becomes an anxiety disorder when our worries get out of control day after day after day, when the worries don't always make sense, when they keep us from doing things we want or need to do, and they make us feel awful. For most people who have an anxiety disorder, "just ignore it" doesn't work.

Sometimes anxiety gave me feelings of dread—warnings that something bad was going to happen. At times I believed worrying was a power that kept me and the people I loved safe. But that wasn't true. Talking with people who understand anxiety has helped me to untangle all my feelings. It's taken me time to develop skills that help me manage anxiety. You can find more information at adaa.org (Anxiety and Depression Association of America).

Whether or not you've struggled with anxiety, you might want to sit down with someone you trust and talk about this book. Decide what you would have done if you'd been me; guess why some of the people acted the way they did; share worries you've had.

To the best of my memory, the vast majority of stories in this book actually happened, though if you ask other people who were there, I'm sure they would remember them differently. I changed everybody's names except my own, guessed at dialogue, moved some events around, and combined some people to make the story smoother.

I took most of the scenes and lines in Alexandra's story directly from the book I was writing in sixth grade—as you can see in the next pages! So how did the story end? I'm not totally sure. When I was ten, I started writing several books, but I never managed to finish one till I was in my mid-twenties. And I didn't publish a book till I was twenty-nine—that was nineteen years after I first declared that I hoped to be a writer. I wanted it to happen much faster! But you know what? It was totally fine. Some things take time. Talents. Friendships. Dreams. Cookies baking in the oven.

If you're like me, you're not perfect either. And that's okay. We don't have to be. I hope you have room to make mistakes. I hope you have friends who get you. And whatever you're going through right now, I hope you hang in there. For me, life gets better and better.

# BEST FRIENDS SCRAPBOOK

Sixth grade! I slept in foam rollers to try to get fabulous 1980s curly hair.

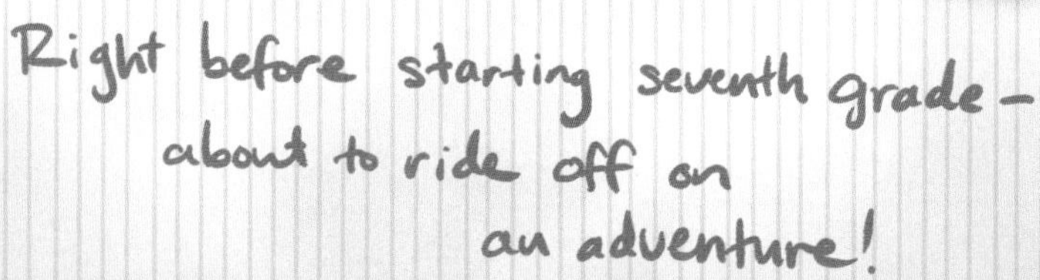

Right before starting seventh grade— about to ride off on an adventure!

LeUyen visits Lagoon.

The roller coaster doesn't scare me...

...until it starts to go up that steep hill.

I can face the "Terroride" with good friends: LeUyen and our editor, Connie.

LeUyen and Connie are determined to win me a prize! Who needs those boys anyway?

6th grade

If this is all your own work, Shannon, it's outstanding

Extra credit
A

1. incredibly good use of detail & description
2. Characterization is excellent
3. very creative idea - fantasy
4. I'm curious what the large room in the manor is about.
5. sentence structure is very good, too.

GIFT OF THE SEA

BY
SHANNON
BRYNER

THE WAVES RUSHED AGAINST HER ANKLES, MAKING THE SUNNY DAY EVEN MORE RELAXING TO ALEXANDRA. THE WATERS RETURNED TO THE OCEAN AND ROLLED BACK TO ALEXANDRA. SHE SIGHED. IF ONLY SHE COULD DO THIS ALL YEAR. DO NOTHING. AFTER BEING AT BORDING SCHOOL FOR THE LAST NINE MONTHS, SHE WAS EGSAUSTED BOTH MENTALLY AND PHYSICALLY. ALEXANDRA WAS GLAD FOR THE BREAK.

good name
nice beginning
good sentences—balanced of long and short - clauses

SOME GIRLS WOULD GIVE ANYTHING TO BE A DAUGHTER OF A MULTI MILLIONARE. WHAT SHE WOULD GIVE TO HAVE NORMAL PARENTS, WITH A NORMAL HOUSE, AND GO TO A NORMAL SCHOOL. OH, HER PARENTS WERE NICE TO HER, THEY LOVED HER AND ALL, BUT THEY NEVER HAD TIME FOR ALEXANDRA. HER PARENTS HAD SENT HER TO YEAR-ROUND BORDING SCHOOL AS SOON AS SHE HAD TURNED FIVE. AND ONLY BY LONG AURGUEMENTS AND A DEAL, WAS ALEXANDRA ABLE TO RETURN TO LONG BEACH FOR A ONE-MONTH SUMMER VACATION.

THIS WAS THE DEAL. ALEXANDRA WOULD RETURN HOME IN JULY. DURING THAT TIME SHE WAS NOT TO COMPLAIN. AND ALEXANDRA WAS NOT TO EXPECT HER PARENTS TO SPEND ALL THEIR TIME WITH HER. AND IF HER PARENTS HAD A TRIP PLANNED IN JULY, THEY WOULD GO ANY WAY. THIS DEAL WAS MADE WITH ALEXANDRA AND HER FATHER; WITHOUT HER MOTHER KNOWING. IF HER MOTHER KNEW, SHE MIGHT INSIST ON STAYING HOME DURING JULY. AND ALEXANDRA'S FATHER DIDN'T WANT THAT.

OH WELL, HER FATHER'S BUISNESS WAS OWNING AN AIRLINE SERVICE. HE HAD HIS PLANES IN EVERY STATE IN THE UNITED STATES. SO HIS LIFE WAS TRAVEL. SO ALEXANDRA COULDN'T BLAME HER FATHER FOR NOT WANTING TO STAY AT LONG BEACH AT THE MOST TRAVELING TIME OF THE YEAR.

ANY WAY, ALEXANDRA ENJOYED BEING ALONE. MOSTLY SHE LIKED BEING ALONE BY THE OCEAN. SHE SUPPOSED THAT THAT WAS THE ONLY RESON THAT SHE COULD STAND BEING AT BORDING SCHOOL DURING ELEVEN MONTHS OF THE YEAR, BECAUSE IT WAS RIGHT ON THE BEACH IN ITALY. THE WAVES BEGAN TO GET HIGHER, ALEXANDRA WAS SOAKING WET. SHE HAD SAT DOWN, BEING LOADED WITH THOUGHTS, AND WAS INTERUPTED BY A LARGE WAVE. good

ALEXANDRA GLANCED AT HER WATCH. IT WAS NEARLY 7:00 AND SHE SHOULD BE GETTING BACK TO THE MANOR. DINNER WAS AT 7:30 AND SHE HAD TO GET CHANGED. ALEXANDRA QUICKLY GRABBED HER SWIM-ROBE AND SLIPPED ON HER SANDELS. SHE HALF JOGGED AND HALF RAN TO REACH THE MANOR IN TIME. THE MANOR WAS SET ON THE BEACH, JUST FAR ENOUGH AWAY FROM THE OCEAN TO BE SAFE FROM THE HIGHEST TIDE. THE MANOR WAS QUITE LARGE. ALEXANDRA'S FATHER HAD INVESTED TWO MILLION DOLLARS IN IT. SHE WENT THROUGH THE BACK GATE, GOT good detail

The first pages of my story with teacher's comments. I guess it was a compliment that she thought I plagiarized it?

good

QUICKLY THROUGH THE GARDEN, AND PUSHED HER WAY THROUGH THE KICHEN, WHICH WAS BUISY WITH MAIDS AND COOKS. ALEXANDRA MADE HER WAY UP THE GREY-MARBLE STAIRCASE, DOWN THE NARROW HALL AND INTO HER ROOM. ALEXANDRA SLIPPED OFF HER SCARLET BATHING SUIT, WHICH LOOKED LOVELY ON HER WITH HER FIRE RED HAIR, HAD A QUICK SHOWER AND PUT ON HER DINNING DRESS. AT LAST THE TWELVE-YEAR-OLD GIRL WAS READY.

Good detail

"WELL, GOOD EVENING ALEXANDRA. DON'T YOU LOOK LOVELY TONIGHT." ALEXANDRA'S MOTHER ADMIRED HER IN HER RED, VELVET GOWN. THE DRESS CAME DOWN TO THE FLOOR, SHOWING ONLY A GLINT OF HER WHITE DRESS SHOES. THE SKIRT HAD SLIGHT FOLDS, MOSTLY AROUND THE BELT. THE COLLAR WAS A 'V' NECK, AND THERE WAS THICK STRAPS, WITH A SOFT RUFFLE.

were

"YES." ALEXANDRA'S PERSONAL MAID AGREED WITH MRS.VANHOFT. "SHE WILL BECOME A BEAUTIFUL WOMAN SOMEDAY."

"TAKES AFTER HER FATHER."MRS. VANHOFT SAID SOFTLY, HALF TO HERSELF AND HALF TO SANDY, THE MAID. ALEXANDRA SIGHED LOWLY. SHE HATED WHEN GROWN-UPS TALKED ABOUT HER LIKE SHE WASN'T THERE.

good

THE DINNER BELL RANG WITH A HIGH-PITCHED SOUND THAT COULD BE HEARD ALL-THROUGH THE MANOR. MR. VANHOFT GRUMBLED AS HE POUNDING DOWN THE STAIRS. HE WAS WEARING BLACK LEATHER, FRESHLY SHINED SHOES. HIS PANTS WERE BLACK, PRESSED AND PLEATED, A WHITE DRESS SHIRT UNDERNEATH A BLACK DRESS COAT TO MATCH HIS PANTS. HE WORE A TIE WITH A GOLD PIN IN THE SHAPE OF THE TAYLOR CUB, IN 1931 THE TAYLOR CUB, OR KNOWN AS THE PIPER CUB, WAS THE BESTKNOWN LIGHT PLANE IN THE UNITED STATES.

Good

"ALEXANDRA, IF I WERE YOU, I WOULD TRY TO STAY OUT OF YOUR FATHERS WAY AS MUCH AS POSSIBLE. I KNOWN IT'S YOUR FIRST NIGHT HOME, BUT HE'S IN A BAD MOOD. YOU CAN BTALK TO HIM PERHAPS TOMARROW."MRS. VANHOFT HURRIDLY WHISPERED TO HER DAUGHTER.

"WHAT'S THE MATTER?" ALEXANDRA HAD ONLY SEEN HER FATHER IN THIS BAD OF A MOOD ONCE BEFORE. ONE OF HIS AIRPORTS HAD CAUGHT ON FIRE AND HAD RUINED ONE OF THE OPPERATING ROOMS. ^ THOUSANDS OF DOLLARS IN DAMAGE OF COMPUTERS AND OTHER GADGETS.

"A BUNCH OF PIOLETS WENT ON STRIKE FOR HIGHER PAY." BONNIE VANHOFT REPLIED,"YOUR FATHER IS WORRIED THAT HE WILL HAVE TO RAISE THEIR SALARY. THAT WOULD MEAN ABOUT $28,000 LESS EVERY YEAR. I DON'T KNOW WHAT HE'S WORRIED ABOUT. HE'S MAKING PLENTY. $28,000 WOULD HARDLY MATTER."

"SIR, TONIGHTS MENU IS NEW YORK STEAK, IDAHO BAKED PATATOES, VIRGINIA HAM, LONG BEACH RAW OYSTERS, AND SOME WASHINGTON APPLES BAKED JUST THE WAY THAT YOU LIKE THEM."

ALEXANDRA COUDN'T HELP LAUGHING. HER FATHER WAS SO IN LOVE WITH THE UNITED STATES THAT HE EVEN HAD THEM FOR DINNER. AND THERE WAS NO SUCH THING AS LONG BEACH OYSTERS.

'THIS IS HOME' THOUGHT ALEXANDRA. 'WHERE EVERY NIGHT MY FATHER FINDS OUT WHAT IS FOR DINNER JUST IN CASE HE DOSENT LIKE WHAT WE'RE HAVING. AND IF HE DOESN'T LIKE IT, THEN HE WILL GO TO THE

I had to cut so much of the story for this book, but you might spy some familiar lines!

# Acknowledgments

LeUyen and Shannon wish to thank—

- The unflappable, always upbeat, fiercely loyal Connie Hsu, our editor extraordinaire, who loves roller coasters but not drop towers.
- Hilary Sycamore and Alex Campbell for their truly inspired coloring, Laura Senechal for the flattening, and Molly Johanson for the amazing design.
- All the First Second and Macmillan folk who have taken such care of these books, including Mark Siegel, Andrew Arnold, Jon Yaged, Allison Verost, Angus Killick, Jen Besser, Jennifer Gonzalez, Jen Edwards, Erin Stein, Morgan Dubin, Shivani Annirood, Lucy Del Priore, Katie Halata, Johanna Kirby, Katie Quinn, Jill Freshney, Alexa Villanueva, and, of course, Connie Hsu, who we already mentioned, but she still deserves to be mentioned twice.
- Our families! Shannon's bulwark Dean, plus in-house focus group Max, Maggie, Wren, and Dinah. Also Mom for the hugs and Dad for giving little me a special folder in his file cabinet to keep my stories. And Uyen's amazing Frenchies at home—Alex, Leo, and Adrien, who are all Uyen needs to keep going. With love to my brothers, Mike and Hank, for being there.
- Trailblazing ladies: Raina Telgemeier, Lisa Brown, Vera Brosgol, and Jenni Holm.
- Shannon's old friends, like Ava Cabey, Shauna Brand, Samantha Stewart, and Rebecca Jensen Maw; and new friends, like Janae Stephenson and her own super trio: Erik, Claire, and Megan.
- Isla Radisich and Mr. Cugley's sixth grade class, and a special shout-out to Morgan in Portland who has been dying for this book to come out.

- All the kids who read *Real Friends* and said, "More please!"
- The booksellers, librarians, and book lovers everywhere who helped match *Real Friends* to readers so that we could make a second.
- And each other—partners in crime, literary other halves, kindred spirits. ("You're the best!" "No, you are!" "No, you!")

**Shannon Hale** is the bestselling author of over thirty books, including the Ever After High series, *Princess Academy* (a Newbery Honor book), and the award-winning graphic memoir *Real Friends*. With her husband Dean, she co-wrote the graphic novels *Rapunzel's Revenge* and *Calamity Jack*, The Unbeatable Squirrel Girl middle grade novels, and the chapter book series The Princess in Black. They live near Salt Lake City, Utah, with four clever children and two fuzzy floofs.

**LeUyen Pham** (lay-win fam) is the *New York Times*–bestselling illustrator of The Princess in Black series with Shannon and Dean Hale and is the creator of *Vampirina Ballerina* with Anne-Marie Pace, now a Disney Junior series. She wrote and illustrated *A Piece of Cake*, *The Bear Who Wasn't There*, and contributed to Mo Willems's Piggy and Elephant series with *The Itchy Book*. She is also the illustrator of *Grace for President* and *The Boy Who Loved Math*. She lives in Los Angeles with her husband, two sons, a cat named Sardine, and a gecko named Kumquat.